The International Holiday & Festival Primer

Book One

The International Holiday & Festival Primer

Book One

David DeRocco, Joan Dundas & Ian Zimmerman

Illustrations: Jan Tufford

© Copyright 1996 FULL BLAST Productions

IN CANADA	IN THE UNITED STATES
FB Productions Box 408 Virgil, Ontario L0S 1T0	FB Productions Box 1297 Lewiston, New York 14092-8297

Reproduction of these materials is permitted only by holders of an original copy for use at the site for which the original purchase was made.

Canadian Cataloguing in Publication Data

DeRocco, David, 1961-
   The international holiday & festival primer

ISBN 1-895451-24-8 (bk. 1)   ISBN 1-895451-25-6 (bk. 2)

1. English language - Textbooks for second language learners.* 2. Readers for new literates. 3. Readers - Holidays. 4. Readers - Festivals. I. Dundas, Joan 1958- . II. Zimmerman, Ian, 1961- . III. Title

PE1128.D473 1996   428.6'4   C96-932413-8

Illustrations: Jan Tufford

ISBN 1-895451-24-8
Printed in Canada

Table of Contents:

	Introduction
Unit 1:	International Women's Day
Unit 2:	Feast of Ridvan (Baha'i)
Unit 3:	Polish Solidarity Day (Poland)
Unit 4:	Salzburg Festival (Austria)
Unit 5:	Ramadan (Muslim)
Unit 6:	Ching Ming Festival (China)
Unit 7:	Black History Month (Canada/U.S.A.)
Unit 8:	Mid-Autumn Festival (various countries)
Unit 9:	Diwali (Hindu)
Unit 10:	Fiesta Patrias (Mexico)
Unit 11:	Easter (Christian)
Unit 12:	Oktoberfest (Germany)
Unit 13:	Earth Day
Unit 14:	Confucius' Birthday/Teacher's Day (Confucian)
Unit 15:	Kartini Day (Indonesia)
Unit 16:	Kupalo Festival (Ukraine)
Unit 17:	Zulu Festival (South Africa)
Unit 18:	Songkran (Buddhist)
Unit 19:	Native American Day (U.S.A.)
Unit 20:	Yom Kippur (Jewish)
Unit 21:	Rizal Day (Phillipines)
Unit 22:	International Day of Peace
Unit 23:	Carnival (Brazil)
Unit 24:	Khordad Sal (Zoroastrian)
Unit 25:	Chinese New Year (various countries)

INTRODUCTION

The International Holiday & Festival Primer is a reproducible ESL/EFL reading-and-discussion text for false beginners, or for true beginners who have already had about eight months of instruction in the language. It offers a number of important design features to make both teaching and learning easier and more enjoyable.

1) Contextualized learning: The short self-contained articles in each unit benefit from a very clear focus that facilitates realistic concentration on inter-related items of vocabulary and grammar that are relevant to the topic and the argumentative purpose.

2) Content that really matters: Each unit examines a holiday celebration that will genuinely interest and inform your students. Readers will learn about the customs and practices of different cultures and religious groups, which serves to promote awareness and understanding of other world communities.

3) Lively journalistic style: Although the passages are carefully limited to an elementary level of language difficulty, their style remains vivid and authentic.

4) Well-balanced exercises: The plentiful exercises offer a good range of integrated activities for each unit--getting the main idea, basic comprehension, finding details, inferences, interpretation and extension of important concepts, vocabulary study, a word puzzle, and a cloze exercise.

5) Illustrations: There is a clear and evocative illustration in each unit; this can be used as a pre-reading exercise, for vocabulary brainstorming, or as the basis for discussion.

6) Answer Key: The text includes a full answer key for every closed-ended question in every unit.

7) Reproducible: Purchase of a copy of the text brings explicit permission to reproduce pages at will, for the use of students at the site where the text is kept.

This package can be used quite simply as it is presented in these pages. In fact, it was carefully planned to be effective in that way. However, resourceful teachers will most likely want to consider one or more of the following suggestions:

- Pre-Activity: Instead of immediately beginning to read the passage, have students start with a discussion to encourage thought about the theme or content of the unit. The picture or title at the head of the unit can be useful in this connection; so can any other realia you can bring into the classroom.

- Order of Exercises: By all means, use all the activities provided for each unit, and allow sufficient time for these to be completed thoroughly (including time for small groups to discuss alternate answers and so on). But build in variety by changing the order in which the exercises are done, and by varying the designation of activities for in-class or at-home assignment.

- Intensity of Work: Be sure to take full advantage of the wide range of different kinds of involvement that these materials offer. At one end of the continuum, for instance, the Interpretation questions can be used to inspire free, creative discussion of themes, values and general ideas. By contrast, at the other end of the continuum, the Word Power exercises provide an excellent foundation for practice in all the detailed and demanding but very important strategies for independent vocabulary development: not just careful contextual reading and word-part analysis, but also dictionary and thesaurus use. Resourceful attention to this kind of varied involvement with the materials will make teaching and learning more enjoyable and more effective, too.

- Post-Activity: Once the class has finished the set of exercises in the text itself, think about rounding off the cycle with a post-activity that clearly links the book and the schoolroom to the wider world. Learners might pursue the theme or content of a given unit by making a bulletin-board collage of their own art work and/or comments, writing letters to a relevant person or institution, going on a visit, watching a video...you will find many ways to reinforce the vocabulary, grammar and content one more time while you also build the self-image of learners as competent language-users for real-life purposes.

- Flexibility: There is no problem with using these units in order, just as provided, but in many circumstances their best application will be as a flexible data-base of content-centered readings that you can access as you see fit. Each term, you'll have different students with different experiences, and so your use of the text will differ as well. With this flexible resource, you can change to meet your students' needs!

International Women's Day

1. In 1872, a woman from Philadelphia, Pennsylvania came up with a wonderful idea. After being saddened by the death of her loving mother, the woman started a letter-writing campaign. In the letters she suggested the idea of setting aside one day annually to honor all mothers across the United States. Today, motherhood is the focus of Mother's Day celebrations held in many countries the second Sunday in May each year.

2. The contribution to society women have made in their roles as mothers is widely recognized. Throughout the course of history, however, women have also made many significant contributions to the world while in other roles.

3. Women are remembered as pioneers and explorers, scientists and doctors, pilots and astronauts, soldiers and politicians, artists, writers, sculptors, painters, inventors and athletes. They have helped build great empires and lived to rule over them as Queens and Presidents. In fact, the greatest stories of history cannot be told without remembering the contribution of the women involved.

4. Today the efforts of working women are remembered every March 8th during International Women's Day. This is a day many countries have set aside to remember the long struggle women have had in achieving civil rights, legal rights and equality.

5. International Women's Day was first declared in the United States in 1910.

The popularity of the holiday grew quickly, and it was soon being celebrated in many other countries, including the former U.S.S.R. and the People's Republic of China.

6   Leading the movement for women's rights in the United States during the 1800s were the suffragettes. Suffragettes were women who felt they should have the same rights as men, especially when it came to the right to vote in elections.

7   Other women like Elizabeth Cady Stanton and Lucretia Mott were opposed to slavery in the U.S. During the early 1800s, a large percentage of all slaves were women, and Stanton and Mott began to speak out against it. When they were often denied the right to speak publicly, they began thinking of ways to improve the status of women. In 1848, they hosted the first women's rights convention in Seneca Falls, New York. This is widely considered to be the beginning of the women's suffrage movement in the U.S.

8   Other events helped rally women's groups together. On March 8, 1857, a group of American women in New York City protesting the terrible working conditions in the garment and textile industry started a revolt that shut down operations. Then in 1909, 18,000 New York garment workers walked off their jobs in protest of backbreaking, low-paying jobs that required them to work 12-14 hours a day, six days a week.

9   Such strikes helped focus attention on the way working women were treated in industrialized American cities. With support from such groups as the American Equal Rights Association, women began to rally across the country. Their efforts led to the first International Women's Day in 1910, and by 1920 all women in the United States were eligible to vote.

10   Today, International Women's Day is marked by celebrations, speeches, and the honoring of women's achievements worldwide.

MAIN IDEAS vs. SUPPORTING DETAILS

The following sentences are either Main Ideas or Supporting Details. Put an "M" beside those that are Main Ideas, and an "S" beside those that are Supporting Details.

1) _____ In 1872, a women from Philadelphia, Pennsylvania started a letter-writing campaign.
2) _____ The greatest stories of history cannot be told without remembering the contributions of the women involved.
3) _____ International Women's Day was first declared in the U.S. in 1910.
4) _____ In 1848, Stanton and Mott hosted the first women's rights conference in Seneca Falls, New York.

UNDERSTANDING WHAT YOU READ

If you can, answer these questions from memory. If you cannot, look back at the article.

1) Why did the Pennsylvanian woman start the letter-writing campaign?

_____

2) When are the efforts of working women remembered?

_____

3) Who led the women's rights movement in the United States?

_____

4) What two events helped rally women's groups together?

_____

REMEMBERING DETAILS

Write TRUE or FALSE under each statement. If the statement is false, write the statement correctly.

1) A Pennsylvanian women started a letter-writing campaign after being denied the right to vote.

_____

2) Women helped build great empires, but were denied the opportunity to rule them as Queens or Presidents.

_____

3) The popularity of International Women's Day grew quickly, but it remained an American celebration.

_____

4) In the U.S., women were denied the right to vote until 1920.

_____

INFERENCES

Based on the article, circle the letter of the best sentence completion.

1) Mott and Stanton hosted the first women's rights convention because...

a) they had been denied the right to speak publicly.
b) they were opposed to slavery.
c) they were the leaders of the suffragette movement in the U.S.
d) they wanted to improve the status of all women.

2) In 1909, women were working in low-paying jobs that required long hours because...

a) they needed the money.
b) women did not have any rights as workers.
c) of the earlier strike in 1857, in which the women's movement lost ground.
d) they were afraid of losing their jobs if they protested.

INTERPRETATION

1) Can you think of a letter-writing campaign that you would like to start? Write a letter to start your campaign.

2) Think of a woman who has made a lasting contribution to society. Write a short composition describing this woman and her accomplishments.

3) Write a short composition contrasting how women were treated in industrialized American cities in the past with how they are treated today. Are there any differences or similarities?

WORD POWER

Circle the letter of the word that means the same as the word on the left.

1) campaign	a) fiasco	b) war	c) project
2) widely	a) spaciously	b) extensively	c) heavily
3) struggle	a) road	b) hassle	c) attempt
4) civil	a) diplomatic	b) moral	c) public
5) rally	a) bring	b) race	c) renew
6) revolt	a) program	b) rebellion	c) renewal

CROSSWORD PUZZLE

ACROSS:
4) Women have made great _____ to society.
8) Many countries have set _____ this day to remember the struggle.
10) Women have lived to _____ over empires.
11) The _____ of working women are remembered every March 8th.
12) The _____ conditions in the garment and textile industry were terrible.
13) She _____ setting aside one day each year to honor all mothers.
15) Other events helped _____ women's groups together.
16) Strikes were held in _____ American cities.

DOWN:
1) The popularity of the holiday grew _____.
2) Today, International Women's Day honors women's _____ worldwide.
3) Stanton and Mott began thinking of ways to improve the _____ of women.
5) In 1872, a women came up with the _____ of a letter-writing campaign.
6) The _____ led the movement for women's rights during the 1800s.
7) They felt they should have the same _____ as men.
9) They also felt that they should be allowed to vote in _____.
14) Stanton and Mott were opposed to _____.

1-5

ANSWER KEY

MAIN IDEAS vs SUPPORTING DETAILS

1) S
2) M
3) M
4) S

UNDERSTANDING WHAT YOU READ

1) The Pennsylvanian woman started the letter-writing campaign to try to get one day each year set aside to honor mothers.
2) The efforts of working women are remembered each March 8th on International Women's Day.
3) The women's rights movement in the United States was lead by the suffragettes. Stanton and Mott were two prominent suffragettes who helped further the cause of women's rights.
4) A revolt in the garment and textile industry in 1857 and a strike in the same industry in 1909 helped to rally women's groups together.

REMEMBERING DETAILS

1) F A Pennsylvanian women started a letter-writing campaign after being saddened by the death of her mother.
2) F Women helped build great empires and lived to rule them as Queens and Presidents.
3) F The popularity of International Women's Day grew quickly, and it was soon being celebrated in many other countries.
4) T

INFERENCES

1) d
2) b

WORD POWER

1) c
2) b
3) b
4) c
5) a
6) b

CROSSWORD PUZZLE

ACROSS: 4) contributions 8) aside 10) rule 11) efforts 12) working 13) suggested 15) rally 16) industrialized

DOWN: 1) quickly 2) achievements 3) status 5) idea 6) suffragettes 7) rights 9) elections 14) slavery

Feast of Ridvan

1 From ancient Greece to modern America, religion has played a very important role in the spiritual lives of millions of people. Since the beginning of recorded history we know that Greeks and Romans, Muslims and Buddhists, Christians, Hindus and Jews and people of dozens of other religious faiths have been worshipping their special God or Gods. Festivals designed to honor these deities are among the holiest events of the year. These celebrations have also become some of the world's best known holidays.

2 While most of the world's most popular religions can be traced back over centuries of worship, there is one rapidly growing religion that got its start less than 200 years ago. The Baha'i Faith is the youngest of the world's independent religions. It is also one of the world's fastest growing, with people from more than 2,000 different ethnic, racial and tribal groups claiming to be Baha'i followers. Across the world, the holiest time of the year for the Baha'i faithful occurs during the Feast of Ridvan.

3 The Feast of Ridvan is known as the King of Festivals to the world's Baha'i community. It is held from April 21st to May 2nd each year to observe the twelve-day period in 1863 when the Baha'i founder Baha'u'llah declared himself as a new messenger of God. To understand the importance of the Feast of Ridvan to Baha'i members, you have to first understand the story

of Baha'u'llah.

4   According to Baha'i scriptures, Baha'u'llah was a nineteenth century prophet. He was born in Persia (modern day Iran) on November 12, 1817 to a very noble family that could link its ancestry back to ancient Persia's greatest dynasties. After declining a successful career with a government ministry, Baha'u'llah chose to devote his energies to helping others. By the early 1840s, he had earned the nickname "Father of the Poor" for his unselfish work.

5   Baha'u'llah was a strong supporter of the Bab, a young merchant who claimed to be the prophet promised in Islamic scripture. When the Bab was executed in 1850, Baha'u'llah began to defend his teachings, and for this he was thrown into a dungeon in Tehran. Upon his release, Baha'u'llah was banished from his homeland, but he continued to spread the word of the Bab.

6   Before his death, the Bab had promised that an even greater prophet would soon be revealed on earth. In 1863, while in exile in Constantinople, Turkey, Baha'u'llah declared that he was in fact the messenger of God foreseen by the Bab. He announced this while standing amongst friends in a garden they later renamed Ridvan, which means "paradise."

7   On the first day, Baha'u'llah made his announcement to family and close friends. On the ninth day, he was joined by others who believed his claim to be God's messenger for the modern age. On the twelfth day, Baha'u'llah left the garden to spread his message.

8   During the Feast of Ridvan, the first, the ninth and the twelfth days of the celebration are especially sacred days. No one works or goes to school on these days, and they honor Baha'u'llah, who died in 1892, with prayer, gatherings, picnics and parties.

MAIN IDEAS vs. SUPPORTING DETAILS

The following sentences are either Main Ideas or Supporting Details. Put an "M" beside those that are Main Ideas, and an "S" beside those that are Supporting Details.

1) _____ Since the beginning of recorded history we know that people of different religions have been worshipping their special God or Gods.
2) _____ The Feast of Ridvan is known as the King of Festivals to the world's Baha'i community.
3) _____ The Bab was a young merchant who claimed he was the prophet promised in Islamic scripture.
4) _____ No one goes to work or school on the first, ninth and twelfth days of the Feast of Ridvan.

UNDERSTANDING WHAT YOU READ

If you can, answer these questions from memory. If you cannot, look back at the article.

1) What are some of the world's best known holidays?

_____

2) When did Baha'u'llah start to promote the Bab's teachings? What happened as a result?

_____

3) Where and when did Baha'u'llah declare that he was a new messenger of God?

_____

4) How is Baha'u'llah honored during the Feast of Ridvan?

_____

REMEMBERING DETAILS

Write TRUE or FALSE under each statement. If the statement is false, write the statement correctly.

1) The Baha'i Faith is over 2,000 years old.

_____

2) The Feast of Ridvan is held annually to celebrate the twelve-day period in 1863 when the Bab declared himself as a new messenger of God.

_____

3) After his release from prison, Baha'u'llah was exiled and stopped spreading the word of Bab.

_____

4) Before his execution in 1850, the Bab promised that a new messenger of God would soon be revealed.

_____

INFERENCES

Based on the article, circle the letter of the best sentence completion.

1) There are many different kinds of religious holidays because...

a) of the use of different calendars: Lunar and Gregorian.
b) of all the different religious faiths and their different Gods.
c) of the different customs of individual countries.
d) of different time zones around the world.

2) Baha'u'llah was a messenger of God because...

a) a prophet was promised in Islamic scriptures.
b) before his death, the Bab promised that a greater prophet would soon be revealed.
c) he declared himself a new messenger of God in 1863.
d) all of the above.

INTERPRETATION

1) What reasons could you imagine led to the Bab's execution?

2) How do you think the people who believed the Bab to be the prophet promised in the Islamic scriptures felt when he was put to death?

3) If someone appeared on the streets of your town claiming to be a messenger from God, what would it take for you to believe that person? Or could you? What would it take for society to believe that person? Or could it?

WORD POWER

Circle the letter of the word that means the same as the word on the left.

1) spiritual	a) bizarre	b) intellectual	c) sacred
2) faiths	a) trusts	b) denominations	c) confidences
3) recorded	a) indicated	b) taped	c) documented
4) messenger	a) prophet	b) postal worker	c) mediator
5) declining	a) refusing	b) rising	c) borrowing
6) foreseen	a) perceived	b) rewarded	c) prophesied

CROSSWORD PUZZLE

ACROSS:
1) Baha'u'llah was a _____ century prophet.
2) The Bab _____ to be the prophet promised in Islamic scriptures.
6) On the _____ day, Baha'u'llah left the garden to spread his message.
7) The Feast of Ridvan is held each year to _____ the declaration by Baha'u'llah.
9) _____ has played an important role in the spiritual lives of millions of people.
11) You must understand the story to understand the _____ of the Feast of Ridvan.
14) Baha'u'llah chose to devote his _____ to helping others.

DOWN:
1) His _____ was "Father of the Poor."
3) Baha'u'llah was thrown into a _____.
4) They honor Baha'u'llah with prayer, _____, picnics and parties.
5) The Baha'i Faith is the _____ of the world's independent religions.
8) Festivals to honor different Gods are amongst the _____ events of the year.
9) There is one _____ growing religion that got its start less than 200 years ago.
10) In 1817, he was born to a very noble family in _____.
12) Ridvan, which means _____, is a garden.
13) Baha'u'llah could link his _____ back to ancient Persia.

2-5

ANSWER KEY

MAIN IDEAS vs SUPPORTING DETAILS

1) S
2) M
3) S
4) S

UNDERSTANDING WHAT YOU READ

1) Some of the world's best known holidays are celebrations that were designed to honor the special God or Gods of the world's dozens of different religious faiths.
2) Baha'u'llah began to promote the Bab's teachings after the Bab's execution in 1850. As a result, Baha'u'llah was thrown into a Tehran prison and then, upon his release, banished from his homeland.
3) On April 21,1863, Baha'u'llah declared that he was a new messenger of God He did this while standing amongst friends in a garden, which was later renamed Ridvan, in Constantinople, Turkey.
4) During the Feast of Ridvan, no one works or goes to school on certain days and they honor Baha'u'llah with prayer, gatherings, picnics and parties.

REMEMBERING DETAILS

1) F   The Baha'i Faith got its start less than 200 years ago.
2) F   The Feast of Ridvan is held annually to celebrate the twelve-day period in 1863 when Baha'u'llah declared himself as a new messenger of God.
3) F   After his release from prison, Baha'u'llah was banished from his homeland but he continued to spread the word of Bab.
4) T

INFERENCES

1) b
2) d

WORD POWER

1) c
2) b
3) c
4) a
5) a
6) c

CROSSWORD PUZZLE

ACROSS: 1) nineteenth 2) claimed 6) twelfth 7) observe 9) religion 11) importance 14) energies

DOWN: 1) nickname 3) dungeon 4) gatherings 5) youngest 8) holiest 9) rapidly 10) Persia 12) paradise 13) ancestry

Polish Solidarity Day

1   On August 31st, 1980, Lech Walesa, an unemployed electrician, stood in front of television cameras set up outside the shipyards in the Polish city of Gdansk. In his hand was a giant pen bearing the picture of another native Pole, Pope John Paul II.

2   When Mr. Walesa signed his name to the Gdansk Agreement, he emerged as the leader of Poland's new, independent labor union--Solidarity. Walesa also became the most recognizable face in the fight against Communism and Soviet influence on Polish politics.

3   Every August 31st since 1980, the people of Poland have celebrated Solidarity Day. However, the events leading up to the first Polish Solidarity Day began right after World War II. At the end of the war, Poland--like most of Eastern Europe--found itself under the influence of the Soviet Communist Bloc. Living conditions in Poland grew harsh, and food, clothing and electricity became luxuries. Polish citizens who openly opposed the Communists were often fired from their jobs, arrested, imprisoned or even killed.

4   Workers across the country also suffered greatly under Communist rule. Long hours, unsafe working conditions and low wages made it very difficult for the average worker to make ends meet. In June 1956, workers in the city of Poznan decided to do something about it. Thousands of workers went on strike, marching through the streets and calling for freedom. Government

troops were called in, and many innocent people were arrested, injured or killed in the riots.

5   After the riots, a new government in Poland promised many reforms. This new era of hope was called "Springtime in October," and Polish people were confident conditions would change.

6   Over the next two decades, however, it was clear the Communist government was doing little to improve life in Poland. Riots at the Gdansk Shipyards in 1970 left hundreds of workers dead or injured. In 1976, an increase in the price of food led to massive riots across Poland. Community leaders realized something had to be done to protect human rights and ensure the safety of Polish workers.

7   On April 29, 1978, Lech Walesa helped form the Baltic Committee for Free and Independent Trade Unions. Their goal was to rally workers into forming a national union. Although he was eventually fired for his union activities, Walesa continued to speak out against the government.

8   By the summer of 1980, minor strikes were breaking out all across Poland. At the Gdansk Shipyards, workers went on strike to protest the firing of both Lech Walesa and Anna Walentynowicz, a woman just five months from retiring. Soon other shipyards in Gdansk and Gdynia joined in the strike. The next day strikers from over 500 factories joined the shipyard workers in a show of solidarity for their cause.

9   With the country on the verge of a total shutdown, the government realized it had to act. On August 23rd, 1980 representatives from the government met with strike leaders. An agreement was finally reached, allowing independent unions to be formed in Poland for the first time. It was signed on August 31, 1980, and Solidarity was formed.

10   Throughout the 1980s, the government continued to harass union leaders. Walesa was actually imprisoned in 1981, and Solidarity was banned from operating. Finally, on April 17, 1989, the union gained full legal status in Poland.

MAIN IDEAS vs. SUPPORTING DETAILS

The following sentences are either Main Ideas or Supporting Details. Put an "M" beside those that are Main Ideas, and an "S" beside those that are Supporting Details.

1) _____ Lech Walesa was an unemployed electrician.
2) _____ Walesa was the leader of the Polish Solidarity Movement.
3) _____ "Springtime in October" was a new era of hope.
4) _____ Solidarity was formed on August 31, 1980.

3-2

UNDERSTANDING WHAT YOU READ

If you can, answer these questions from memory. If you cannot, look back at the article.

1) What happened to the Polish citizens who openly opposed the Communists?

_____

2) When did the movement towards Solidarity get its start?

_____

3) What does the author mean by "working conditions and low wages make it very difficult for the average worker to make ends meet"?

_____

4) What happened to Lech Walesa after he helped form the Baltic Committee for Free and Independent Trade Unions?

_____

REMEMBERING DETAILS

Write TRUE or FALSE under each statement. If the statement is false, write the statement correctly.

1) Pope John Paul II was at the Gdansk Shipyards on August 31, 1980.

_____

2) After World War II, food, clothing and electricity became necessities.

_____

3) After the riots, the Communists improved life in Poland.

_____

4) On August 23, 1980, government representatives met with strike leaders to reach an agreement to end the strike.

_____

3-3

INFERENCES

Based on the article, circle the letter of the best sentence completion.

1) Lech Walesa used a pen, bearing a picture of Pope John Paul II, to sign the Gdansk Agreement because...

a) he was a Roman Catholic.
b) the Pope was a famous native Pole.
c) he wanted to defy the Communists.
d) it was his lucky pen.

2) Walesa became the most recognizable face in the fight against Communism and Soviet influence on Polish politics because...

a) he was imprisoned for his views.
b) he signed the Gdansk Agreement.
c) he formed the Baltic Committee for Free and Independent Trade Unions.
d) all of the above.

INTERPRETATION

1) Discuss with a partner the symbolism of Walesa's use of the pen with the Pope's picture on it to sign the Gdansk Agreement.

2) Write a timeline for the development of Solidarity.

3) Discuss why you think living conditions got worse in Poland after World War II.

WORD POWER

Circle the letter of the word that means the same as the word on the left.

1) bearing	a) carrying	b) tolerating	c) displaying
2) union	a) combination	b) club	c) association
3) influence	a) domination	b) wing	c) prestige
4) era	a) century	b) period	c) year
5) ensure	a) guarantee	b) arrange	c) insecure
6) rally	a) mobilize	b) invigorate	c) challenge

CROSSWORD PUZZLE

ACROSS:

4) In 1981, Solidarity was _____ from operating.
5) In June, 1956, thousands of workers went on _____.
6) Anna Walentynowicz was just five months from _____.
8) Walesa became the most _____ face in the fight against Communism.
10) Walesa helped form the _____ Committee for Free and Independent Trade Unions.
13) After the riots, a new government in Poland promised many _____.
15) In his hand was a giant pen bearing the picture of another _____ Pole.

DOWN:

1) Throughout the 1980s, the government continued to _____ union leaders.
2) Poland was on the _____ of a total shutdown.
3) An increase in the price of food led to _____ riots across Poland.
6) Their goal was to _____ workers into forming a national union.
7) Living conditions in Poland grew _____.
9) Walesa _____ as the leader of Solidarity.
11) It became _____ the Communist government was doing little to improve life.
12) Polish people were _____ conditions would change.
14) Workers across the country also _____ greatly under Communist rule.

3-5

ANSWER KEY

MAIN IDEAS vs SUPPORTING DETAILS

1) S
2) M
3) S
4) M

UNDERSTANDING WHAT YOU READ

1) Polish citizens who openly opposed the Communists were often fired from their jobs, arrested, imprisoned or even killed.
2) The movement towards Solidarity started in 1956 when workers in the city of Poznan decided to do something about unsafe working conditions and low wages, which made it difficult to make ends meet. Thousands of workers went on strike, marching through the streets and calling for freedom.
3) The author means that it was difficult for Poles to earn enough money to pay for the basic necessities of life.
4) Lech Walesa was eventually fired after he helped form the Baltic Committee for Free and Independent Trade Unions.

REMEMBERING DETAILS

1) F   Lech Walesa held a pen in his hand bearing the picture of Pope John Paul II at the Gdansk Shipyards on August 31, 1980.
2) F   After World War II, food, clothing and electricity became luxuries.
3) F   After the riots, the Communists promised many reforms, but it became clear that they were doing little to improve life in Poland.
4) T

INFERENCES

1) b
2) d

WORD POWER

1) c
2) c
3) a
4) b
5) a
6) a

CROSSWORD PUZZLE

ACROSS: 4) banned 5) strike 6) retiring 8) recognizable 10) Baltic 13) reforms 15) native

DOWN: 1) harass 2) verge 3) massive 6) rally 7) harsh 9) emerged 11) clear 12) confident 14) suffered

Salzburg Festival

1   When his son was born in 1756, Austrian Leopold Mozart named the boy Wolfgang Amadeus and vowed to teach him all he knew about composing music. By the time Wolfgang was six years old, he had already performed for the royal courts of Paris, London and most of Europe. Soon, the entire world came to know this talented young musical genius by his now-famous last name, Mozart.

2   World renowned Austrian composer Wolfgang Amadeus Mozart died in 1791 at age 35. But in his short life, he created some of the world's most beautiful and popular pieces of music. From the time he was a boy, Mozart showed an amazing ability to play violin, organ and harpsichord. However, his real skills were as a composer of fine music.

3   As an eight-year-old child, Mozart composed his first symphony. Over the years, he continued to produce everything from operas to choral suites. Today he is remembered as one of the most gifted musical artists in history.

4   Unfortunately for Mozart, while he was alive he was far less famous in his hometown than he was in the rest of Europe. After his death, the people of Salzburg did little to honor him. In fact, this beautiful city in west-central Austria became more famous for its Alpine resorts and spas than as the birthplace of Mozart.

5   That mistake was corrected in 1906 when the city organized the first ever

Salzburg Festival. From the time it began in late July to the time it ended in late August, the Salzburg Festival was a celebration of classical music that paid special tribute to the city's most famous citizen. Today in Austria and much of Europe, the Salzburg Festival is simply called the Mozart Festival in honor of his lasting contribution to music.

6   On stages and in concert halls across Salzburg, the festival plays host to a wide variety of musical events. Composers from around the world travel to Salzburg, as do world-class musicians, conductors, singers and most of all, music lovers.

7   Since Mozart composed such a wide variety of musical pieces, visitors to the Salzburg Festival can expect to hear many different styles of music being performed at various venues across the city. At the Franziskanerkirche, where Sunday masses have traditionally included a full orchestra and choir, Mozart's finest church music can be heard echoing through the halls. Other sacred works by Mozart can be heard at the Abbey of St. Peter's or the Salzburg Cathedral, with its 4,000-pipe organ.

8   Two famous Austrian theaters--the Festspielhaus and the Landestheater--also play host to events during the Salzburg Festival. Because of their size and sound quality, most of the operas and orchestral pieces written by Mozart are performed on these stages. Here visitors can listen to operas such as *The Marriage of Figaro* and *Don Giovanni*, or Mozart's famous ballet, *Les Petits Riens*.

9   Along with such other famous names as Beethoven, Bach, Rossini and Chopin, Mozart is still one of the world's best loved classical composers. But since the Salzburg Festival began in 1906, nowhere is he more loved than in the city where he was born.

MAIN IDEAS vs. SUPPORTING DETAILS

The following sentences are either Main Ideas or Supporting Details. Put an "M" beside those that are Main Ideas, and an "S" beside those that are Supporting Details.

1) _____ Leopold Mozart vowed to teach his son all about composing music.
2) _____ Mozart was a young musical genius.
3) _____ The Salzburg Festival is a celebration of classical music that pays special tribute to Mozart.
4) _____ Mozart composed a wide variety of musical pieces.

UNDERSTANDING WHAT YOU READ

If you can, answer these questions from memory. If you cannot, look back at the article.

1) As what is Mozart primarily remembered?

___

2) During his lifetime, where was Mozart famous? Where was he not famous?

___

3) By what name is the Salzburg Festival now known?

___

4) Where is Mozart's music performed during the Salzburg Festival?

___

REMEMBERING DETAILS

Write TRUE or FALSE under each statement. If the statement is false, write the statement correctly.

1) Leopold Mozart failed in his attempts to teach his son how to compose music.

___

2) Mozart composed his first symphony when he was six years old.

___

3) Salzburg recognized Mozart as a famous classical composer in 1906.

___

4) During the Salzburg Festival, most of Mozart's operas are performed at the Franziskanerkirche.

___

INFERENCES

Based on the article, circle the letter of the best sentence completion.

1) Mozart is remembered as one of the world's most gifted musical artists because...

a) he produced everything from operas to choral suites.
b) he had an amazing ability to play a variety of musical instruments.
c) he is loved as a composer of some of the world's most beautiful and popular music.
d) all of the above.

2) Composers, musicians, conductors, singers and music lovers travel from around the world to the Salzburg Festival because...

a) it is the only music festival of its calibre in the world.
b) of the great variety and quality of Mozart's musical compositions.
c) of Salzburg famous Alpine resorts and spas.
d) of the 4,000-pipe organ at Salzburg Cathedral.

INTERPRETATION

1) Discuss with a partner why you think Mozart, while alive, was not famous in his hometown.

2) What types of music do you enjoy? Do you enjoy classical music? Discuss your musical preferences with your classmates.

3) Do you think it is a good idea for parents to begin training their children in a specific discipline, like Leopold Mozart did, at a very early age? Discuss the benefits and drawbacks.

WORD POWER

Circle the letter of the word that means the same as the word on the left.

1) vowed	a) swore	b) promised	c) married
2) talented	a) skilled	b) showy	c) energetic
3) genius	a) young person	b) intelligent person	c) energetic person
4) renowned	a) measured	b) gifted	c) famous
5) gifted	a) talented	b) generous	c) stable
6) venues	a) streets	b) locations	c) churches

CROSSWORD PUZZLE

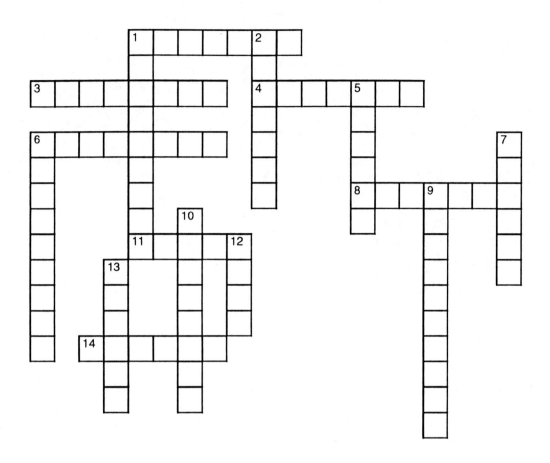

ACROSS:
1) Mozart created some of the world's most _____ pieces of music.
3) Wolfgang Amadeus Mozart was an _____.
4) He is remembered as one of the most gifted musical _____ in history.
6) His skills were as a _____ of fine music.
8) Mozart's finest church music can be heard _____ through the halls.
11) After his _____, the people of Salzburg did little to honor him.
14) Mozart is Salzburg's most _____ citizen.

DOWN:
1) Mozart had _____ for royalty by the time he was six years old.
2) Mozart showed an _____ ability to play violin, organ and harpsichord.
5) Many different _____ of music are performed at the Salzburg Festival.
6) Mozart remains one of the world's best loved _____ composers.
7) *The Marriage of* _____ is one of Mozart's operas.
9) Most of Mozart's _____ pieces are performed at two famous Austrian theaters.
10) In 1906, the city organized the first ever _____ Festival.
12) The Salzburg Festival plays _____ to a wide variety of musical events.
13) Nowhere is _____ more loved than in the city where he was born.

ANSWER KEY

MAIN IDEAS vs SUPPORTING DETAILS

1) S
2) M
3) M
4) S

UNDERSTANDING WHAT YOU READ

1) Mozart is remembered primarily as a composer of fine classical music.
2) During his lifetime, Mozart was famous in most of Europe, but not in Salzburg, Austria.
3) The Salzburg Festival is now known as the Mozart Festival.
4) During the Salzburg Festival, Mozart's music is performed in concert halls, churches and Austrian theaters.

REMEMBERING DETAILS

1) F   Leopold Mozart was very successful in his attempts to teach his son how to compose music. His son is famous as a composer.
2) F   Mozart composed his first symphony when he was eight years old.
3) T
4) F   During the Salzburg Festival, most of Mozart's operas are performed at the Festspielhaus and the Landestheater.

INFERENCES

1) d
2) b

WORD POWER

1) b
2) a
3) b
4) c
5) a
6) b

CROSSWORD PUZZLE

ACROSS: 1) popular 3) Austrian 4) artists 6) composer 8) echoing 11) death 14) famous

DOWN: 1) performed 2) amazing 5) styles 6) classical 7) *Figaro* 9) orchestral 10) Salzburg 12) host 13) Mozart

Ramadan

1   One of the world's largest and most influential religions is called Islam, a name which means "submission to God." The approximately one billion members of Islam, called Muslims, are found in many parts of the world, but primarily in the Middle East, Northern Africa and parts of Asia. Some newly-independent republics of the former Soviet Union are predominantly Muslim.

2   While Islam is monotheistic--worshipping only one god, Allah--Muslims also celebrate the legacy of Muhammad, their last prophet and the one they consider Allah's one true messenger. It was to Muhammad that Allah communicated the teachings of Islam's holy book, the Koran. To this day, Muslims consider this man with the greatest respect; this can be seen in their proclamation known as the Shahadah: "There is no God but Allah, and Muhammad is his Prophet."

3   The Shahadah is the first in what are known as the Five Pillars of Islam. These "pillars" are the principles that govern the lives of Muslims. The other four are; prayer, charity, fasting and pilgrimage. The most intensive form of the Fourth Pillar, fasting, takes place once every year in the Islamic calendar; this period of fasting is known as Ramadan.

4   Even though the Koran was recited to Muhammad over a period of years, Muslims observe as their holy month the ninth lunar month. This is the month when Muhammad received his

first revelation from Allah. The beginning of this month is marked by the appearance of the new moon.

5   Each day during Ramadan, Muslims are forbidden from eating, drinking and smoking from the appearance of the sun's light in the morning sky to its disappearance in the evening. After dark, they have only moderate amounts, usually eating a few dates with water to drink. The evening prayer is then recited.

6   Only pregnant women, very sick people and children are exempted from the fast, and compensation is to be made by fasting on other days or by feeding the poor.

7   One night of Ramadan is considered especially holy. This "Night of Power" usually falls on the twenty-seventh day of Ramadan, and marks the night of Allah's first communication to Muhammad. It is observed by the performing of special prayers; some people will pray all night. After that, the mosques--the Muslim places of worship--may be illuminated, and entertainers put on a variety of performances. On this night, a second meal may be eaten before dawn.

8   The final breaking of the fast comes with the beginning of the tenth month as signalled by the new moon. The end of Ramadan is celebrated by a feast and, after prayers, the traditional custom is to put on new clothes and visit friends.

9   For Muslims it is hoped that the twenty-nine or thirty days of abstinence will lead to greater knowledge of one's place in God's world. The fasting person is more likely to appreciate his or her frailty and reliance on God. He or she may also approach those who are truly poor and hungry with greater compassion and charity, having experienced this hunger themselves. The life that is returned to after Ramadan is enriched by God's work.

MAIN IDEAS vs. SUPPORTING DETAILS

The following sentences are either Main Ideas or Supporting Details. Put an "M" beside those that are Main Ideas, and an "S" beside those that are Supporting Details.

1) _____ Some newly-independent republics of the former Soviet Union are predominantly Muslim.
2) _____ The Five Pillars of Islam are the principles that govern the lives of Muslims.
3) _____ The "Night of Power" is considered especially holy.
4) _____ The life returned to after Ramadan is enriched by God's work.

UNDERSTANDING WHAT YOU READ

If you can, answer these questions from memory. If you cannot, look back at the article.

1) What does Islam mean?

_____

2) What are the Five Pillars of Islam?

_____

3) What is forbidden during Ramadan?

_____

4) Which night of Ramadan is considered especially holy?

_____

REMEMBERING DETAILS

Write TRUE or FALSE under each statement. If the statement is false, write the statement correctly.

1) The Shahadah proclaims "there is no God but Allah."

_____

2) During Ramadan Muslims will eat only during daylight hours.

_____

3) The "Night of Power" falls on the last night of Ramadan.

_____

4) The fasting person is more likely to appreciate his or her frailty and reliance on God.

_____

INFERENCES

Based on the article, circle the letter of the best sentence completion.

1) Islam is one of the world's largest and most influential religions because...

a) they are found in many parts of the world.
b) some of the newly-independent republics of the former Soviet Union are Muslim.
c) there are approximately one billion members.
d) Islam means "submission to God."

2) Ramadan is the most intensive of the Five Pillars of Islam because...

a) praying on one's knees each night is difficult.
b) it is indeed difficult to not eat from sunrise to sundown for one month.
c) of the great feast on the last day.
d) entertainment is provided in the mosque.

INTERPRETATION

1) Brainstorm with your classmates possible reasons why some newly-independent republics of the Soviet Union are Muslim.

2) Imagine you have been fasting for a month, as in Ramadan. What food would you plan to eat on the last day? With a partner, plan a menu for your feast.

3) Do you believe fasting leads to greater knowledge of one's spiritual self? Write a short composition to support your opinion.

WORD POWER

Circle the letter of the word that means the same as the word on the left.

1) influential	a) effective	b) controversial	c) powerful
2) proclamation	a) declaration	b) advertisement	c) broadcast
3) forbidden	a) prohibited	b) forgiven	c) encouraged
4) illuminated	a) inspired	b) lighted	c) instructed
5) signalled	a) indicated	b) observed	c) celebrated
6) hardship	a) enjoyment	b) suffering	c) fasting

CROSSWORD PUZZLE

ACROSS:

2) The end of Ramadan is _____ by a feast.
3) The life returned to after Ramadan is _____ by God's work.
6) Muhammad is considered to be the Muslim's last _____.
8) Islam means _____ to God.
9) The _____ is the first of the Five Pillars of Islam.
12) Muslims are _____ from eating, drinking and smoking during daylight hours.
15) Ramadan requires 29 to 30 days of _____.

DOWN:

1) Mosques are Muslim places of _____.
4) The "Night of Power" marks the night of Allah's first _____ to Muhammad.
5) Ramadan is an annual period of _____.
6) Muslims are found _____ in the Middle East.
7) The _____ custom is to put on new clothes and visit friends.
10) A second meal may be eaten later before _____.
11) Fasting is considered a _____ for Muslims.
13) The evening prayer is then _____.
14) The final _____ of the fast comes with the beginning of the tenth month.

5-5

ANSWER KEY

MAIN IDEAS vs SUPPORTING DETAILS

1) S
2) M
3) M
4) M

UNDERSTANDING WHAT YOU READ

1) Islam means submission to God.
2) The Five Pillars of Islam are the Shahadah, prayer, charity, fasting and pilgrimage.
3) Eating, drinking and smoking are forbidden from sunrise to sunset during Ramadan.
4) The "Night of Power" or the 27th day of Ramadan is considered especially holy.

REMEMBERING DETAILS

1) F   The Shahadah proclaims "there is no God but Allah, and Muhammad is his Prophet."
2) F   During Ramadan Muslims fast during the day and after dark have only moderate amounts to eat and drink, usually a few dates with water.
3) F   The "Night of Power" falls on the 27th day of Ramadan.
4) T

INFERENCES

1) c
2) b

WORD POWER

1) c
2) a
3) a
4) b
5) a
6) b

CROSSWORD PUZZLE

ACROSS: 2) celebrated 3) enriched 6) prophet 8) submission 9) Shahadah 12) forbidden 15) abstinence

DOWN: 1) worship 4) communication 5) fasting 6) primarily 7) traditional 10) dawn 11) hardship 13) recited 14) breaking

Ching Ming Festival

1 Thousands of years ago, during the Chou Dynasty in China (1122-221 BC), the noble Lord of Tsin gathered his closest friends together and set off on foot on a perilous journey. Misfortune quickly fell upon the travellers. Lost in a strange land, they soon grew cold, tired and close to starving. It was decided that the Lord of Tsin must be saved. To spare the Lord's life, one of his closest friends made the supreme sacrifice: he asked to be killed, so that the others could eat him and avoid dying.

2 When the group was finally rescued, the Lord of Tsin was so grateful for his brave companion's unselfish act he decided to honor him. The Lord declared that once a year, people should set aside a day to pay tribute to the memory of dead friends and relatives who had lived their lives in such noble fashion.

3 This is just one of the many legends surrounding the Chinese festival known as Ching Ming (or Qing Ming). Another theory is that the festival had its start in the Han Dynasty between 202 BC and 220 AD. Regardless of when it began, Chinese people around the world continue to celebrate Ching Ming on April 5th or 6th each year. It arrives around the third day of the third moon, 105 days after the winter solstice has ended.

4 Many ancient customs and traditions are followed during the Ching Ming Festival. As winter begins to fade away, Chinese people start to celebrate the promise of the coming spring during

the Li Chum festival. When spring officially arrives, it is time for Ching Ming, which when translated into English means "pure and bright."

5   According to ancient tradition, all the fires in Chinese kitchens are allowed to burn out three days before Ching Ming begins. During this period very little food is eaten, and it is Chinese custom to serve cold food to family and guests.

6   During the early part of Ching Ming, people visit the graves of family members and ancestors. This is a time to honor the dead and "sweep their tombs." All graves and burial grounds are swept of fallen leaves, cleared of weeds, decorated with sprigs of willow and replanted with flowers or trees. New paint may be applied to grave markers, and repairs are completed on burial mounds and altars.

7   Though Ching Ming is a day to remember those who have died, it is not supposed to be a sad occasion. Both the rich and the poor make offerings as a way of remembering departed souls. Huge feasts are prepared and eaten, while similar meals are placed at gravesides so the dead may snack on the spiritual part of the food.

8   In another ancient custom, bags of paper money are put on family altars, and prayers are whispered. The money is then taken outside and burned. This is done in order to free the souls of the dead who have come to visit with their families during Ching Ming, and to provide them with money in the afterworld. Other ancient customs include playing Chinese football, flying kites and setting off firecrackers.

9   In many cities in modern China, Ching Ming has now become a day of patriotism. Memorial wreaths are placed at the gravesides of revolutionary heroes who helped the Communist cause. It is a new tradition in the ongoing celebrations of the Ching Ming Festival.

MAIN IDEAS vs. SUPPORTING DETAILS

The following sentences are either Main Ideas or Supporting Details. Put an "M" beside those that are Main Ideas, and an "S" beside those that are Supporting Details.

1) _____ Lost in a strange land, the Lord of Tsin and his friends soon grew cold, tired and close to starving.
2) _____ The Lord of Tsin decided to honor his brave companion by designating a day to pay tribute to the memory of dead friends and relatives.
3) _____ Many ancient customs and traditions are followed during the Ching Ming Festival.
4) _____ In modern China, many cities celebrate Ching Ming as a day of patriotism.

UNDERSTANDING WHAT YOU READ

If you can, answer these questions from memory. If you cannot, look back at the article.

1) When did the Ching Ming Festival start?

_____

2) What does Ching Ming mean?

_____

3) What is done during the early part of Ching Ming?

_____

4) Why are bags of paper money put on family altars and then taken outside and burned?

_____

REMEMBERING DETAILS

Write TRUE or FALSE under each statement. If the statement is false, write the statement correctly.

1) The Lord of Tsin sacrificed his life so that his fellow travellers could live.

_____

2) Ching Ming is a festival of sadness.

_____

3) Meals are placed at the gravesides of the dead so that they can snack on the spiritual part of food.

_____

4) In modern China, memorial wreaths are placed at the gravesides of friends and relatives.

_____

INFERENCES

Based on the article, circle the letter of the best sentence completion.

1) One of the Lord of Tsin's friends decided to sacrifice his own life because...

a) he was tired and could no longer continue.
b) the journey was too perilous.
c) he was worried that their leader was in danger.
d) he was ordered to by the Lord of Tsin.

2) This festival is called Ching Ming, which means "pure and bright," because...

a) it happens each year as winter begins to fade into spring.
b) in the springtime the earth is renewed and everything is new and fresh.
c) the souls of the departed are considered to be "pure and bright."
d) of the sacrifices made by revolutionary heroes who helped the Communist cause.

INTERPRETATION

1) Why do you think the Chinese allow their kitchen fires to burn out three days before Ching Ming? With a partner, generate a list of possible reasons. Share your list with the rest of the class.

2) What type of food would make a good spiritual snack for the dead? Discuss your ideas with a partner.

3) According to one Ching Ming custom, bags of paper money are burned for the dead to use in the afterworld. Write a short composition describing how you would spend money in the afterworld.

WORD POWER

Circle the letter of the word that means the same as the word on the left.

1) perilous	a) long	b) dangerous	c) unstable
2) supreme	a) ultimate	b) insane	c) selfish
3) grateful	a) thankful	b) upset	c) obliged
4) noble	a) grandiose	b) unusual	c) honorable
5) patriotism	a) flag-waving	b) national pride	c) celebration
6) ongoing	a) moving	b) annual	c) continuing

CROSSWORD PUZZLE

ACROSS:
1) _____ wreaths are placed at the gravesides of revolutionary heroes.
2) The Lord of Tsin lived during the Chou _____.
3) The money is then taken outside and _____.
5) One friend decided to _____ his own life in order to save the Lord of Tsin.
6) Meals are placed at the _____ of the dead.
9) Ching Ming arrives 105 days after the winter _____ has ended.
11) Another _____ custom has people place bags of paper money on family altars.
13) This is done to provide the dead with money in the _____.

DOWN:
1) Along the way _____ fell upon the group of travellers.
3) At this time, repairs are completed on _____ mounds and altars.
4) The Chinese festival known as Ching Ming is based on many _____.
5) This is a time to honor the dead and to _____ their tombs.
7) Ching Ming is not supposed to be a _____ occasion.
8) Chinese people celebrate the _____ of the coming spring during Li Chum.
10) Ching Ming means "pure and bright" when _____ into English.
12) During Ching Ming, people visit the _____ of family members.

6-5

ANSWER KEY

MAIN IDEAS vs SUPPORTING DETAILS

1) S
2) M
3) M
4) M

UNDERSTANDING WHAT YOU READ

1) One legend has the Ching Ming Festival starting during the Chou Dynasty between 1122 and 221 BC, while another theory has the beginning of the Ching Ming Festival in the Han Dynasty between 202 BC and 220 AD.
2) Ching Ming means "pure and bright."
3) During the early part of Ching Ming, people visit the graves of family members and ancestors. This is a time to honor the dead and "sweep their tombs." All graves and burial grounds are swept of fallen leaves, cleared of weeds, decorated with sprigs of willow and replanted with flowers or trees. New paint may be applied to grave markers, and repairs are completed on burial mounds and altars.
4) Bags of paper money are put on family altars and then taken outside and burned so as to free the souls of the dead and to provide them with money in the afterworld.

REMEMBERING DETAILS

1) F   Lord Tsin did not sacrifice his life so that his fellow travellers could live. One of Lord Tsin's friends sacrificed his life so that Lord Tsin and the others on their trip could live.
2) F   Though Ching Ming is a day to remember those who have died, it is not supposed to be a sad occasion.
3) T
4) F   Memorial wreaths are placed at the gravesides of revolutionary heroes who helped the Communist cause.

INFERENCES

1) c
2) c

WORD POWER

1) b
2) a
3) a
4) c
5) b
6) c

CROSSWORD PUZZLE

ACROSS: 1) memorial 2) Dynasty 3) burned 5) sacrifice 6) gravesides 9) solstice 11) ancient 13) afterworld

DOWN: 1) misfortune 3) burial 4) legends 5) sweep 7) sad 8) promise 10) translated 12) graves

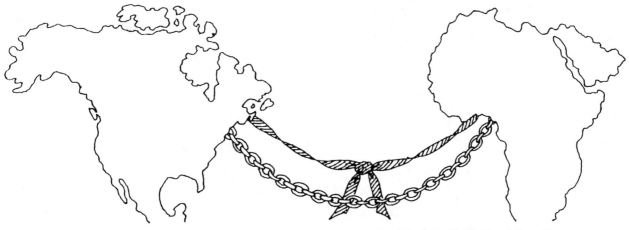

FROM THE VAST HERITAGE AND CULTURE OF THE DISTANT PAST, THE SLAVERY AND STRUGGLES OF THE RECENT PAST AND AN UNWAVERING HOPE FOR THE FUTURE COMES A NEW PEOPLE, A NEW CULTURE AND HERITAGE.

"UNCONQUERED AND UNCONQUERABLE"

Black History Month

1   "If a race has no history, if it has no worthwhile tradition, it becomes a negligible factor in the thought of the world, and it stands in danger of being exterminated."

2   These words were spoken by Carter G. Woodson in 1926, the year that Negro History Week was established. As Negro History Week has grown to become Black History Month, Woodson's words have continued to be the celebration's guiding principle.

3   Carter G. Woodson was a scholar of African American history, and became known as "The Father of Black History." In 1915, he founded the Association for the Study of Negro Life and History, or ASNLH, in order to promote the contribution of Africans and African Americans to the history of the world. At about the same time, another African American scholar, Booker T. Washington, was promoting African American education through Negro Health Week. This week proved to be a popular success, and led to the idea of a week to mark African American history.

4   The first Negro History Week was declared by Woodson's Association in Washington, D.C. Set for the second week in February, the week was to include both the birthday of Abraham Lincoln, the American President who signed the Emancipation Proclamation to free black slaves, and the birthday of Frederick Douglass.

5   Douglass was an African American who escaped the bonds of slavery in the

early 1800s, and went on to become a prominent spokesman for the anti-slavery movement. He is considered a hero to African Americans for the personal risk taken by his outspoken position--at any time before Emancipation in 1863, he could have been captured and returned to the cruelty of slavery. Even after Emancipation, Douglass devoted his life to the promotion of civil rights for African Americans.

6 The first Negro History Week included exhibits of contributions made by African American soldiers, of black church history, and of the social and economic advancements made by African American people after the abolition of slavery.

7 The influence of Negro History Week is difficult to measure, but since its inception African Americans have made great gains in American society. In the 1960s, the Civil Rights Movement allowed African American voices to be raised more strongly than ever; at this time, too, Negro History Week unofficially became Black History Month; this new observance was recognized by the United States government in 1976, the year of America's two hundredth birthday. Black History Month has also been recognized in countries outside the United States, including Canada.

8 To this day, Carter G. Woodson's ASNLH is an influential force in the observance of Black History Month. Every year a specific theme for the month is declared by the Association, and special kits outlining the nature of each year's observance are sent to schools, churches, libraries, ASNLH branches and other organizations. Activities are planned which draw attention to African and African American accomplishments throughout history. For both adults and children, courses are offered in black history and lectures, demonstrations and exhibits of African and African American art and culture take place.

9 Black History Month has probably grown beyond its founder's original vision of educating African Americans as to their own history. Today, people of all races participate in the enlightenment that Black History Month has to offer.

MAIN IDEAS vs. SUPPORTING DETAILS

The following sentences are either Main Ideas or Supporting Details. Put an "M" beside those that are Main Ideas, and an "S" beside those that are Supporting Details.

1) _____ Negro History Week has grown to become Black History Month.
2) _____ Carter G. Woodson became known as "The Father of Black History."
3) _____ African Americans have made great gains in American society since the inception of Negro History Week.
4) _____ People of all races participate in the enlightenment that Black History Month has to offer.

UNDERSTANDING WHAT YOU READ

If you can, answer these questions from memory. If you cannot, look back at the article.

1) Who was Carter Woodson?

_____

2) What did Booker T. Washington do around 1915?

_____

3) What significance did Abraham Lincoln have on Negro History Week?

_____

4) What influence does the ASNLH have on the celebration of Black History Month each year?

_____

REMEMBERING DETAILS

Write TRUE or FALSE under each statement. If the statement is false, write the statement correctly.

1) Negro History Week was established in 1915 by Booker T. Washington.

_____

2) Frederick Douglass devoted his life to the promotion of civil rights for African Americans.

_____

3) During the 1960s, Negro History Week officially became Black History Month.

_____

4) Carter Woodson's ASNLH plays a minor role in the present-day celebration of Black History Month.

_____

INFERENCES

Based on the article, circle the letter of the best sentence completion.

1) Woodson became known as "The Father of Black History" because...

a) his speech in 1926 became the guiding principle of Black History Week.
b) he was a scholar of African American history.
c) he founded the ASNLH.
d) all of the above.

2) Black History Month has probably grown beyond its founder's original vision because...

a) today all races participate in its activities.
b) each year there is a special theme set by the ASNLH.
c) there are exhibits of African and African American art and culture.
d) it is now recognized in countries outside of the United States.

INTERPRETATION

1) Make a chronological timeline for the development of Black History Month.

2) In a short composition, explain what Carter Woodson's words mean to you.

3) Why do you think the influence of Negro History Week has been hard to measure ?

WORD POWER

Circle the letter of the word that means the same as the word on the left.

1) negligible	a) unimportant	b) indifferent	c) careless
2) exterminated	a) forgotten	b) exonerated	c) destroyed
3) personal	a) physical	b) selfish	c) human
4) voices	a) opinions	b) clamor	c) noise
5) grown	a) sprouted	b) improved	c) evolved
6) vision	a) sight	b) dream	c) viewpoint

CROSSWORD PUZZLE

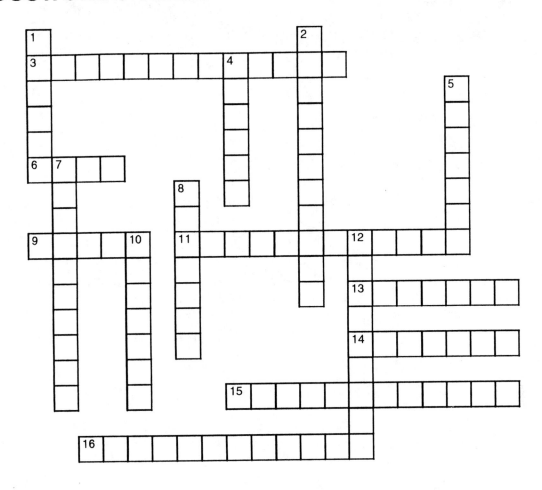

ACROSS:
3) Black History Month offers _____ to people of all races.
6) Activities are planned which _____ attention to their accomplishments.
9) Frederick Douglass escaped the _____ of slavery in the early 1800s.
11) In the 1960s Negro History Week _____ became Black History Month.
13) Douglass could have been captured and returned to the _____ of slavery.
14) Negro Health Week proved to be a _____ success.
15) Abraham Lincoln signed the _____ Proclamation to free black slaves.
16) The ASNLH promotes the _____ of Africans and African Americans to history.

DOWN:
1) Black History Month has probably grown _____ its founder's original vision.
2) Woodson's ASNLH is _____ in the observance of Black History Month.
4) Special kits outlining the _____ of each year's observance are distributed.
5) If a race has no _____, it becomes a negligible factor in the thought of the world.
7) Black History Month has also been _____ in countries outside the United States.
8) In 1915, Woodson _____ the ASNLH.
10) Carter G. Woodson was a _____ of African American history.
12) Things have changed since the _____ of Negro History Week.

7-5

ANSWER KEY

MAIN IDEAS vs. SUPPORTING DETAILS

1) S
2) M
3) M
4) S

UNDERSTANDING WHAT YOU READ

1) Carter Woodson was a scholar of African American history who founded the ASNLH in 1915. He became known as "The Father of Black History."
2) Around 1915 Booker T. Washington promoted African American education through Negro Health Week. This week led to the idea of a week to mark African American history.
3) Abraham Lincoln, whose birthday falls in the second week of February, signed the Emancipation Proclamation to free black slaves. Negro History Week is celebrated the second week in February, in part, to pay honor to this man.
4) Each year the ASNLH sets a specific theme for Black History Month and special kits based on this theme are sent to schools, churches, libraries, ASNLH branches and other organizations.

REMEMBERING DETAILS

1) F   Negro History Week was established in 1926 by the ASNLH. Negro Health Week was started by Booker T. Washington in 1915.
2) T
3) F   During the 1960s, Negro History Week unofficially became Black History Month.
4) F   To this day, Carter Woodson's ASNLH is an influential force in the observance of Black History Month.

INFERENCES

1) d
2) a

WORD POWER

1) a
2) c
3) a
4) a
5) c
6) b

CROSSWORD PUZZLE

ACROSS: 3) enlightenment 6) draw 9) bonds 11) unofficially 13) cruelty 14) popular 15) Emancipation 16) contribution

DOWN: 1) beyond 2) influential 4) nature 5) history 7) recognized 8) founded 10) scholar 12) inception

Mid-Autumn Festival

1   Under the glow of a bright September moon, children gather together in groups across Asia. Munching away on their tasty mooncakes, some carrying paper lanterns and lighting firecrackers, they sit and listen to ancient tales while searching the skies for the mysterious lady in the moon. It is the fifteenth day of the eighth moon, and time for the Mid-Autumn Festival.

2   In China, Korea, Vietnam, Japan, Taiwan and other countries where large Asian communities can be found, the Mid-Autumn Festival is a time for great celebration. On the full moon nearest to September 15th, around the time when harvest festivities are being held in many other nations, the Mid-Autumn Festival is held to honor the ancient Moon Goddess.

3   There are many different folk tales explaining the appearance of the ancient Moon Goddess. But according to one popular legend, the story begins with Hou Yih, an officer in the Chinese emperor's bodyguard nearly 3,000 years ago. When 10 suns appeared in the sky threatening to burn the earth, the emperor ordered Hou Yih to shoot nine of them. After completing the task, Hou Yih was awarded with a pill that would make him immortal. When his beautiful wife Chang-O found the pill, she swallowed it. She was quickly swept up to the moon to live forever, and today her beauty continues to shine in the radiant glow of the moon.

4   In modern China, the Mid-Autumn Festival is a national holiday. Family reunions are part of festival traditions,

with great feasts and gift-giving also being a big part of the celebrations. The most popular food served during the festival is mooncakes, a thin round pastry shell filled with a variety of sweet ingredients. The round shape of the cake is both a symbol of the full moon and of the unity of the family. Mooncakes are often presented as gifts to people who have travelled great distances to visit friends and family.

5   In both cities and country villages across Asia, many of the celebrations are geared towards children. Parades are often led through the streets, with children carrying moon-shaped paper lanterns and candles. Giant dragons made of paper and cloth make their way along the parade route, and firecrackers are often lit in celebration.

6   Perhaps the most widely held tradition during the Mid-Autumn Festival is the viewing of the moon. Millions of people gather on beaches, on hilltops, up mountainsides and in open spaces to gaze at the brilliance of the moon.

7   In Japan, this custom of moon-viewing is called "tsukimi." Huge moon-viewing festivals are held in places like Hyakkaen Garden, Mukojima and Tokyo. On the island of Osawa, hundreds of boats gather together to watch the moon. Many Japanese celebrate the festival by placing offerings of cooked vegetables and moon-viewing dumplings on a table as gifts to the spirit of the moon. In Taiwan, where the festival is called Tiong-chiu Choeh, people picnic on mountainsides to get the best view of the full autumn moon.

8   Many people believe that the moon is brightest during the time of the Mid-Autumn Festival. In the moonlight, they are often inspired to pray to the Moon Goddess for good luck, family unity, protection and the promise of love.

MAIN IDEAS vs. SUPPORTING DETAILS

The following sentences are either Main Ideas or Supporting Details. Put an "M" beside those that are Main Ideas, and an "S" beside those that are Supporting Details.

1) _____ Under the glow of a bright September moon, children gather together in groups across Asia.
2) _____ The Mid-Autumn Festival is held on the full moon nearest September 15th to honor the ancient Moon Goddess.
3) _____ The emperor asked Hou Yih to shoot nine of the ten suns that had appeared in the sky.
4) _____ Mooncakes are often given as gifts to people who have travelled great distances to visit friends and family.

UNDERSTANDING WHAT YOU READ

If you can, answer these questions from memory. If you cannot, look back at the article.

1) How do children celebrate the Mid-Autumn Festival?

_____

2) Who is the mysterious lady of the moon?

_____

3) What is the most popular food served during the Mid-Autumn Festival?

_____

4) What is the most widely held tradition during the Mid-Autumn Festival?

_____

REMEMBERING DETAILS

Write TRUE or FALSE under each statement. If the statement is false, write the statement correctly.

1) The Mid-Autumn Festival is held on the first day of the eighth moon.

_____

2) The emperor rewarded Chang-O by giving her a pill that would make her immortal.

_____

3) The mooncake's round shape symbolizes the purity of the spirit.

_____

4) In both cities and villages, parades are held that feature moon-shaped paper lanterns, candles and giant dragons made of cloth and paper.

_____

INFERENCES

Based on the article, circle the letter of the best sentence completion.

1) Mooncakes are the most popular food during the festival because...

a) they are tasty pastries filled with a variety of sweet ingredients.
b) their round shape symbolizes the round shape of the moon.
c) so many of them are given as gifts to friends and family
d) they are easy to eat and easy to carry to the Mid-Autumn Festival.

2) Many of the celebrations are geared towards children because...

a) this is the one time of the year that they are allowed to stay up late.
b) family unity is one of the themes of the Mid-Autumn Festival.
c) they carry the paper lanterns in the parades.
d) they are especially fond of mooncakes.

INTERPRETATION

1) Write a short composition on your reasons why many cultures place an emphasis on the full moon.

2) Imagine that you are one of the children that has gathered to search the skies for the mysterious lady in the moon. Describe your experience in as much detail as possible and then share it with a partner.

3) The symbolism behind mooncakes has been given, but what do you think the symbolism is behind the use of paper lanterns?

WORD POWER

Circle the letter of the word that means the same as the word on the left.

1) tasty	a) savory	b) bland	c) pasty
2) mysterious	a) mystical	b) obscure	c) beautiful
3) folk tales	a) tall tales	b) legends	c) family memories
4) immortal	a) without morals	b) perish	c) deathless
5) radiant	a) cheerful	b) luminous	c) warm
6) gaze at	a) watch	b) take in	c) pray to

CROSSWORD PUZZLE

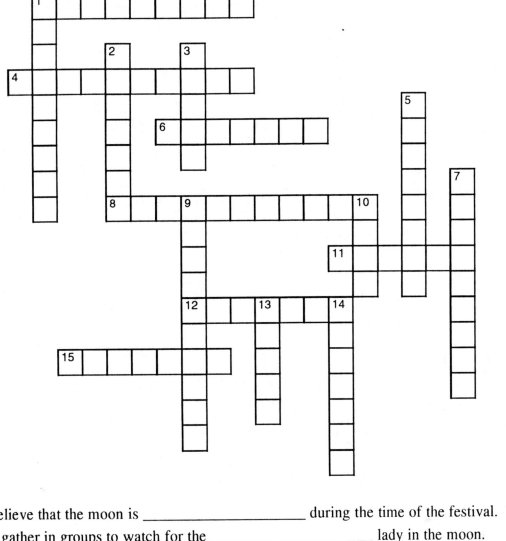

ACROSS:
1) People believe that the moon is _____ during the time of the festival.
4) Children gather in groups to watch for the _____ lady in the moon.
6) According to one _____ legend, the story begins with Hou Yih.
8) Ten suns appeared in the sky _____ to burn the earth.
11) The Mid-Autumn Festival is a national holiday in _____ China.
12) Hou Yih was _____ with a pill that would make him immortal.
15) The most widely held tradition is the _____ of the moon.

DOWN:
1) Hou Yih was an officer in the Chinese emperor's _____.
2) The Mid-Autumn Festival takes place on the full moon _____ to September 15th.
3) The festival is held to _____ the ancient Moon Goddess.
5) Many celebrations are geared towards _____.
7) The most popular food served during the festival are _____.
9) There are many different folk tales _____ the appearance of the Moon Goddess.
10) Today Chang-O's beauty continues to shine in the radiant _____ of the moon.
13) The _____ shape of the mooncake is symbolic.
14) Giant _____ are made of paper and cloth.

8-5

ANSWER KEY

MAIN IDEAS vs SUPPORTING DETAILS

1) S
2) M
3) S
4) M

UNDERSTANDING WHAT YOU READ

1) To celebrate the Mid-Autumn Festival children gather in groups and, while watching for the mysterious lady in the moon, eat mooncakes, carry paper lanterns and light firecrackers.
2) According to one popular legend, the Moon Goddess is Hou Yih's wife, Chang-O, who swallowed an immortality pill given to her husband. She was then swept up to the moon to live forever.
3) The most popular food served during the Mid-Autumn Festival is mooncakes.
4) The most widely held tradition during the Mid-Autumn is the viewing of the moon, which is done all across Asia.

REMEMBERING DETAILS

1) F The Mid-Autumn Festival is held on the fifteenth day of the eighth moon.
2) F The emperor rewarded Hou Yih by giving him a pill that would make him immortal.
3) F The mooncake's round shape symbolizes the full moon and the unity of the family.
4) T

INFERENCES

1) b
2) b

WORD POWER

1) a
2) a
3) b
4) c
5) b
6) a

CROSSWORD PUZZLE

ACROSS: 1) brightest 4) mysterious 6) popular 8) threatening 11) modern 12) awarded 15) viewing

DOWN: 1) bodyguard 2) nearest 3) honor 5) children 7) mooncakes 9) explaining 10) glow 13) round 14) dragons

Diwali

1   Even though it may mean different things to Hindus in different regions, Diwali is as important to Hindus as Christmas is to Christians. Diwali is also a meaningful celebration to the Sikh community.

2   The word Diwali is adapted from the Sanskrit word "Deepawali," which means a row or cluster of lights. Diwali itself is known as the Festival of Lights. It is an annual observance held during the autumn month the Hindus call Karthika. Common to the celebrations held throughout the Hindu world is the presence of a display of lights.

3   In India, Diwali is a time to worship the goddess of wealth, who is known as Lakshmi. Houses are prepared for her arrival by being completely cleaned and white-washed. On the night of the festival, the houses are illuminated by many lights, whether candles, oil lamps or electric bulbs. It is not uncommon for a house to display rows of oil lamps on its roof, on its outer walls and in its yard or garden. It is believed that Lakshmi will not give her blessing to a home that is not illuminated for her welcome.

4   As in festivals of other cultures, fireworks are lit to celebrate this special night. But as well as delighting the spectators, the fireworks are believed to chase away evil spirits. Almost every house participates in the fireworks display, and the noisy and colorful celebration illuminates whole

streets and villages well into the night.

5 In some villages there is also a big communal bonfire of firewood, brush, and even oil-soaked rags, which send the fire leaping high into the sky. As the fire rises it is accompanied by drum beats, and the spectators around the fire share in the joyous occasion.

6 Diwali also holds special significance for people in the business community. On this day businesses close their account books for the previous year. A new account book is placed before a picture of Lakshmi to receive her blessing, in the hopes that the goddess of wealth will multiply profits in the coming year.

7 Some Hindu communities elsewhere celebrate Diwali somewhat differently. In Malaya, for instance, the day begins at four in the morning with a ritual bath, and a lamp is lit for the worship of Lakshmi. Later in the day, people dress in new clothes and visit their friends and neighbors. Exchanging gifts is also customary. Great feasts are prepared and eaten, and the day ends with a display of rows of oil lamps.

8 Sikhs also celebrate Diwali, though of course it does not carry the same religious meaning as the Hindu celebration. Instead Sikh Diwali is in honor of Guru Hargobind, the sixth guru. It is said that the Sikhs originally illuminated the Golden Temple at Amritsar to mark the Guru's release from prison in 1620, and to this day Sikh celebrants still light the Temple with candles and electric lights on Diwali. Sikh Diwali is also a time to display Sikh treasures, light fireworks, and exchange gifts.

9 In Diwali we can see how customs may change and be adapted by different people to serve different purposes. Yet for all these people Diwali remains an impressive and important occasion.

MAIN IDEAS vs. SUPPORTING DETAILS

The following sentences are either Main Ideas or Supporting Details. Put an "M" beside those that are Main Ideas, and an "S" beside those that are Supporting Details.

1) _____ In India on the night of the Diwali festival houses are illuminated by many lights.
2) _____ Common to the celebrations held throughout the Hindu world is the presence of a display of lights.
3) _____ In India, Diwali holds special significance for people in the business community.
4) _____ In Diwali we can see how customs may change and be adapted by different people to serve different purposes.

UNDERSTANDING WHAT YOU READ

If you can, answer these questions from memory. If you cannot, look back at the article.

1) What does Diwali mean?

_____

2) Who is Lakshmi?

_____

3) What special significance does Diwali hold for people in the business community?

_____

4) Who do Sikhs honor when they celebrate Diwali?

_____

REMEMBERING DETAILS

Write TRUE or FALSE under each statement. If the statement is false, write the statement correctly.

1) Hindus illuminate their homes in an effort to keep Lakshmi away.

_____

2) The bonfires held in some villages are very sad and somber affairs.

_____

3) Common to all Hindu celebrations of Diwali is a display of lights.

_____

4) For Sikhs Diwali has the same meaning as it does for Hindus.

_____

INFERENCES

Based on the article, circle the letter of the best sentence completion.

1) Some Hindus celebrate Diwali differently because...

a) the Hindu population is spread throughout many regions.
b) Malaya does not have electricity.
c) Sikhs do not worship Lakshmi.
d) fireworks are forbidden in India.

2) Diwali is known as the Festival of Lights because...

a) in India houses are illuminated by many lights.
b) in some villages there is a big communal bonfire.
c) in all regions lights are used as part of the celebrations.
d) in Malaya a lamp is lit to worship Lakshmi.

INTERPRETATION

1) How do the different regions celebrate Diwali? Make a list of their similarities and differences.

2) Write a short composition describing the significance of Lakshmi to the Hindus and Sikhs.

3) For what "different purposes" has Diwali been adapted?

WORD POWER

Circle the letter of the word that means the same as the word on the left.

1) cluster	a) collection	b) throng	c) crowd
2) common	a) simple	b) public	c) customary
3) communal	a) traditional	b) cultural	c) shared
4) significance	a) importance	b) energy	c) origins
5) ritual	a) important	b) ceremonial	c) formal
6) impressive	a) stable	b) memorable	c) energetic

CROSSWORD PUZZLE

ACROSS:
1) The word Diwali is adapted from the _____ word "Deepawali."
4) Hindus believe Lakshmi will give her _____ to illuminated homes.
9) _____ is the month in which Diwali is celebrated.
11) An _____ book is placed before a picture of Lakshmi to receive her blessing.
12) Sikhs originally celebrated Diwali to mark the Guru's _____ from prison.
13) For Sikhs Diwali does not carry the same _____ meaning as for Hindus.
16) The spectators around the fire share in the _____ occasion.

DOWN:
2) Diwali is an _____ celebration.
3) On the night of the _____, the houses are illuminated by many lights.
5) The goddess of _____ is known as Lakshmi.
6) _____ are lit to celebrate this special night.
7) _____ gifts is customary.
8) Diwali remains an impressive and _____ occasion.
10) They hope the goddess of wealth will _____ their profits.
14) The festival ends with the display of rows of _____ lamps.
15) Guru Hargobind was the _____ guru.

ANSWER KEY

MAIN IDEA vs SUPPORTING DETAILS

1) S
2) M
3) M
4) M

UNDERSTANDING WHAT YOU READ

1) Diwali means a row or cluster of lights.
2) Lakshmi is the goddess of wealth.
3) The special significance Diwali holds for people in the business community is that on Diwali businesses close their account books for the previous year and then a new account book is placed before a picture of Lakshmi to receive her blessing. It is hoped that the goddess of wealth will multiply profits in the coming year.
4) Sikh Diwali is in honor of Guru Hargobind, the sixth guru.

REMEMBERING DETAILS

1) F   People illuminate their homes in an effort to attract Lakshmi. They want the goddess to bless their homes.
2) F   The bonfires are a joyous occasion.
3) T
4) F   The Sikh version of Diwali does not carry the same religious meaning as the Hindu celebration.

INFERENCES

1) a
2) c

WORD POWER

1) a
2) c
3) c
4) a
5) b
6) b

CROSSWORD PUZZLE

ACROSS: 1) Sanskrit 4) blessing 9) Karthika 11) account 12) release 13) religious 16) joyous

DOWN: 2) annual 3) festival 5) wealth 6) fireworks 7) exchanging 8) important 10) multiply 14) oil 15) sixth

Fiesta Patrias

1   It has been said that it would be impossible to estimate the number of fiestas held each year in Mexico; there are both religious and patriotic festivals, and every city, village and neighborhood has its own annual celebration. But whatever the reason, all are invited to take part, and on the anniversary of Mexico's independence from the Spanish, the whole country joins in.

2   The festival of Independence Day in Mexico is called Fiesta Patrias. This patriotic fiesta is celebrated over the course of a week, but September fifteenth and sixteenth are the most significant dates of the festival.

3   September fifteenth is the anniversary of the beginning of Mexico's eleven year fight for independence from Spanish rule. On that night in the year 1810, Father Miguel Hidalgo y Costilla urged the people of the town of Dolores to revolt against Mexico's Spanish government.

4   Father Hidalgo's call to arms is re-enacted every year during Fiesta Patrias. In every town and city, the streets and the town square are decorated with lights the color of the Mexican flag: red, green and white. Brightly colored decorations and confetti fill the streets, and bands provide musical accompaniment to the festival spirit.

5   As eleven o'clock approaches, people gather to wait for the appearance of the town's mayor. From a balcony

10-1

overlooking the town square, the mayor plays the part of Father Hidalgo, and cries out the "Grito de Dolores," the ("Cry of Dolores") as the Father's inspirational speech has come to be known. The townspeople echo the mayor's cries, sometimes yelling "Viva Mexico" (Long Live Mexico") for up to an hour.

6   In some historically significant towns --Dolores itself, for instance--elaborate productions recreate heroic events from the battle for independence.

7   In Mexico City, the capital of Mexico, the country's president stands on the balcony of the National Palace to declare the "Grito." Then he rings the Liberty Bell, believed to be the same bell rung by Father Hidalgo on September fifteenth in 1810. The city then erupts into a great clamor of yelling, car horns, factory whistles and party noisemakers. The festivities continue into the night with displays of fireworks.

The day of September sixteenth is Independence Day. In the larger cities, the day is marked by military parades; in small towns the parade's participants are children. Girls dress in colorful skirts, while boys wear white suits with bright blankets; on their heads they wear the wide-brimmed hat of Mexico, the sombrero. Traditionally, a boy is chosen to represent Father Hidalgo, and a girl is chosen to represent the fatherland of Mexico. In the town square girls walk in pairs in a big circle, while boys walk in pairs in the opposite direction, each shyly eyeing the other as they pass. The general merriment continues throughout the day and night with more displays of fireworks, noise and dancing.   8

For the Mexican people, many of whom are poor, Fiesta Patrias is a time to live outside of everyday rules, and to celebrate alongside other Mexican people. Fiesta Patrias is a festival for all Mexican people, and this makes it a special time for all.   9

MAIN IDEAS vs. SUPPORTING DETAILS

The following sentences are either Main Ideas or Supporting Details. Put an "M" beside those that are Main Ideas, and an "S" beside those that are Supporting Details.

1) _____   It is impossible to estimate the number of fiestas held each year in Mexico.
2) _____   Father Hidalgo's call to arms is re-enacted every year during Fiesta Patrias.
3) _____   As eleven o'clock approaches, people gather to wait for the appearance of the town's mayor.
4) _____   Fiesta Patrias is a festival for all Mexican people.

UNDERSTANDING WHAT YOU READ

If you can, answer these questions from memory. If you cannot, look back at the article.

1) How long was Mexico's fight for independence from Spanish rule?

_____

2) By what name is Father Hidalgo's inspirational speech known?

_____

3) What is the Liberty Bell?

_____

4) When is Independence Day and how is it celebrated?

_____

REMEMBERING DETAILS

Write TRUE or FALSE under each statement. If the statement is false, write the statement correctly.

1) Fiesta Patrias is celebrated annually on September fifteenth and sixteenth.

_____

2) Father Hidalgo y Costilla urged the people of Dolores to revolt against Spanish rule with the "Grito de Dolores."

_____

3) September fifteenth is Independence Day.

_____

4) All Mexican people are well-off.

_____

INFERENCES

Based on the article, circle the letter of the best sentence completion.

1) Mexico celebrates Fiesta Patrias because...

a) it is just another one of numerous fiestas held each year in Mexico.
b) it is the anniversary of its independence from the Spanish.
c) the inspirational speech, the "Grito de Dolores," is re-enacted.
d) its president rings the Liberty Bell.

2) Mexico's president rings the Liberty Bell on the balcony of the National Palace because...

a) Mexicans enjoy noisy fiestas.
b) he lives in Mexico City and is therefore unable to travel to Dolores.
c) all can see him ring the bell if he stands on the balcony.
d) it is believed to be the same bell used by Father Hidalgo in 1810.

INTERPRETATION

1) Discuss with a partner reasons why you think Mexico sought independence from Spanish rule.

2) Write a short inspirational speech on a subject of your own choosing. Practice your speech with a partner and then present it to your class.

3) Make a list of the similarities and differences between how September fifteenth is celebrated in Mexico City and Dolores.

WORD POWER

Circle the letter of the word that means the same as the word on the left.

1) estimate	a) prize	b) calculate	c) value
2) annual	a) yearly	b) frequent	c) monthly
3) fiesta	a) trial	b) celebration	c) display
4) urged	a) rushed	b) drove	c) encouraged
5) echo	a) reflect	b) repel	c) repeat
6) merriment	a) fun	b) annoyance	c) display

CROSSWORD PUZZLE

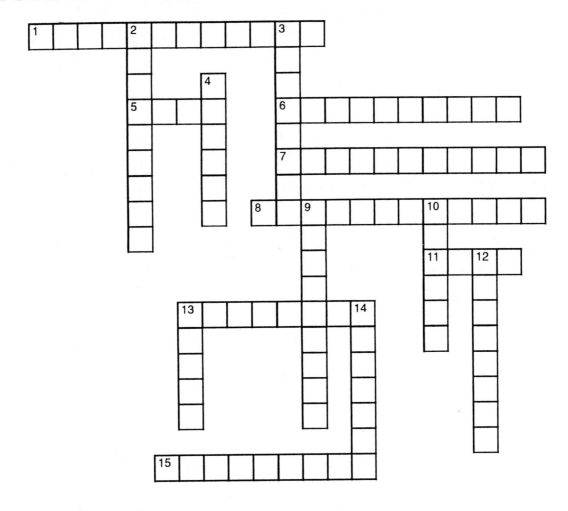

ACROSS:
1) It is the anniversary of Mexico's _____ from the Spanish.
5) Mexico's fight for independence from Spanish _____ began on Sept. 15th, 1810.
6) A girl is chosen to represent the _____ of Mexico.
7) The _____ echo the mayor's cries for up to an hour.
8) There are elaborate productions in some _____ significant towns.
11) Father Hidalgo's call to _____ is re-enacted every year.
13) The wide-brimmed hat of Mexico is the _____.
15) Fiesta is also a time for Mexicans to celebrate _____ other Mexican people.

DOWN:
2) Fiesta Patrias is a _____ fiesta that is celebrated over the course of a week.
3) Brightly colored decorations and _____ fill the streets.
4) Father Hidalgo urged the people to _____ against Mexico's Spanish government.
9) The day of September _____ is Independence Day.
10) The city then erupts into a great _____.
12) In the larger cities, the day is marked by _____ parades.
13) The boys and girls _____ eye each other as they pass each other.
14) Fiesta is a time to live _____ of everyday rules.

10-5

ANSWER KEY

MAIN IDEAS vs SUPPORTING DETAILS

1) S
2) M
3) S
4) M

UNDERSTANDING WHAT YOU READ

1) Mexico's fight for independence from Spanish rule lasted eleven years.
2) Father Hidalgo's inspirational speech is known as the "Grito de Dolores" or the "Cry of Dolores."
3) The Liberty Bell is the bell rung by Mexico's president on September fifteenth, and it is believed to be the same bell rung by Father Hidalgo in 1810.
4) Independence Day is on September sixteenth and it is marked by parades, displays of fireworks, noise and dancing.

REMEMBERING DETAILS

1) F   Fiesta Patrias is celebrated over the course of a week, but September fifteenth and sixteenth are the most significant dates of the festival.
2) T
3) F   September sixteenth is Independence Day.
4) F   Many Mexican people are poor.

INFERENCES

1) b
2) d

WORD POWER

1) b
2) a
3) b
4) c
5) c
6) a

CROSSWORD PUZZLE

ACROSS: 1) independence 5) rule 6) fatherland 7) townspeople 8) historically 11) arms 13) sombrero 15) alongside

DOWN: 2) patriotic 3) confetti 4) revolt 9) sixteenth 10) clamor 12) military 13) shyly 14) outside

Easter

1   Many of the world's most festive holiday events are planned by the people of a nation to celebrate special occasions held only in their country. Other holidays are so rich in history and tradition that they are shared and celebrated by people in many nations around the world. In such cases, people of different races, cultures and religions observe the same holiday.

2   Easter is one of the most commonly observed international holidays in the world. In the West, Easter is held on the first Sunday after the full moon that appears on or following March 21. For Eastern Orthodox churches, it usually falls several weeks later: in the East they follow the Julian rather than the Gregorian calendar, which is followed in the West. What is truly surprising, however, is the different reasons why people around the world celebrate the Easter season.

3   To some, it is the day on the calendar that signals the end of winter and the arrival of the spring sun: a good reason to celebrate! To others, Easter is a truly sacred event and one of the holiest religious holidays of the year. But whatever the reasons behind the celebration, there is no question that Easter customs, traditions, rituals and images have been around for thousands of years.

4   Next to Christmas Day, Easter is by far the most important religious holiday to Christian worshippers around the world. The annual observance marks the anniversary of

the crucifixion of Jesus Christ upon the cross and his return to life, events of nearly 2,000 years ago. Christians commonly refer to the miracle of Christ's return from the dead as the "Resurrection." For Christians, this is a time of joyous celebration. Since the original discovery of Christ's Resurrection by Mary Magdalene, Christians have thought this to be a true sign that there is eternal life.

5   The arrival of Easter Sunday brings an official end to Lent, a forty day period of self-denial. This period of personal denial and fasting is meant to test Christians' faith and show their love for God. The final week of Lent is called Holy Week, which includes Palm Sunday (the day Jesus arrived in Jerusalem) and Good Friday (the day of his crucifixion). This is a week of religious rites and ceremonies leading up to Easter Sunday.

6   While Easter celebrations are rich with Christian symbols, there are also a number of pagan or non-religious associations. The word Easter, for example, may have originated in Saxony many centuries ago. Easter was the name of the Saxons' goddess of spring and fertility. Others believe Easter is named after an ancient Germanic goddess named Ostara, whose companion was a wild hare, or rabbit.

7   During the nineteenth century, German immigrants introduced the Easter hare to North America. Today, the Easter "Bunny" is a major symbol of North American Easter celebrations. Children decorate eggs and hope the Easter Bunny will deliver candy and chocolate to them on Easter morning.

8   Despite the spread of such non-religious symbols, Easter remains a holy Christian holiday celebrating the new beginning found in Christ's Resurrection. This promise of new life is also symbolized by the spring weather that returns with Easter to renew the earth each year.

MAIN IDEAS vs. SUPPORTING DETAILS

The following sentences are either Main Ideas or Supporting Details. Put an "M" beside those that are Main Ideas, and an "S" beside those that are Supporting Details.

1) _____ Some holidays are so rich in history and tradition that they are shared and celebrated by people in many nations around the world.
2) _____ In the East, Easter usually falls several weeks later than in the West.
3) _____ Easter celebrations are rich with Christian symbols.
4) _____ The Easter Bunny is a major symbol of North American Easter celebrations.

UNDERSTANDING WHAT YOU READ

If you can, answer these questions from memory. If you cannot, look back at the article.

1) When is Easter?

_____

2) What are the different reasons why people celebrate Easter?

_____

3) What is Lent?

_____

4) Where did the Easter Bunny originate?

_____

REMEMBERING DETAILS

Write TRUE or FALSE under each statement. If the statement is false, write the statement correctly.

1) Easter is celebrated on the same day by all Christians.

_____

2) For Christians, Easter is a time of somber reflection.

_____

3) Holy Week is a week of religious rites and ceremonies leading up to Easter Sunday.

_____

4) The Easter Bunny delivers toys to children on Easter morning.

_____

INFERENCES

Based on the article, circle the letter of the best sentence completion.

1) To some, Easter is the holiest religious holiday because...

a) it happens at the same time as spring.
b) it marks the anniversary of Christ's crucifixion upon the cross.
c) it signifies the new beginning found in Christ's Resurrection.
d) it is more important than Christmas.

2) There are a number of pagan associations to Easter because...

a) of the migration of German immigrants to the U.S.
b) of the migration of English immigrants to Canada.
c) Easter has a tradition dating back that far in time.
d) children love getting candy and chocolates from the Easter Bunny.

INTERPRETATION

1) Can you think of any other ways Easter is celebrated around the world?

2) Why does the Easter Bunny bring candy and chocolates to children on Easter Sunday? Can you think of more appropriate gifts?

3) Another non-religious symbol associated with Easter is the Easter Egg. Brainstorm possible reasons for this association with a partner.

WORD POWER

Circle the letter of the word that means the same as the word on the left.

1) festive	a) joyous	b) irreverent	c) religious
2) commonly	a) seldom	b) universally	c) lately
3) signals	a) marks	b) alarms	c) lights
4) miracle	a) sensation	b) sight	c) phenomenon
5) eternal	a) immortal	b) long	c) sacred
6) companion	a) master	b) friend	c) chaperon

CROSSWORD PUZZLE

ACROSS:

3) The arrival of Easter Sunday brings an _____ end to Lent.
4) This promise of new life is symbolized by the spring _____.
6) The annual observance marks the anniversary of the _____ of Jesus Christ.
7) Easter is _____ in history and tradition.
9) The Easter _____ is celebrated for different reasons.
10) Mary Magdalene was the _____ discoverer of Christ's return to life.
11) Spring weather brings the _____ of new life.
12) Children _____ eggs and hope the Easter Bunny will deliver candy.
13) Easter is a _____ religious holiday to Christians.
16) Easter celebrations are rich with Christian _____.

DOWN:

1) Some people believe Easter is named after a _____ named Ostara.
2) The miracle of Christ's return to life is known as the _____.
5) Easter is one of the most important religious holidays to Christian _____.
8) Ostara's companion was a wild _____.
14) Holy Week is a week of religious _____ and ceremonies.
15) Lent is a period of personal _____ and fasting.

11-5

ANSWER KEY

MAIN IDEAS vs SUPPORTING DETAILS

1) S
2) S
3) S
4) M

UNDERSTANDING WHAT YOU READ

1) In the West, Easter is held on the first Sunday after the full moon that appears on or following March 21st. For Eastern Orthodox churches, it usually falls several weeks later. In the East they follow the Julian rather than the Gregorian calendar, which is followed in the West.
2) To some people, Easter is the day on the calendar that signifies the beginning of spring. To others, Easter is one of the holiest religious holidays of the year.
3) Lent is a forty day period of personal denial and fasting that is meant to test a person's faith and show their love for God.
4) The Easter Bunny originated with a Germanic goddess named Ostara, whose companion was a wild rabbit. The Easter Bunny was then introduced to North America by German immigrants.

REMEMBERING DETAILS

1) F   Easter is usually celebrated on different days in the West and in the East.
2) F   For Christians, Easter is a time of joyous celebration.
3) T
4) F   The Easter Bunny delivers candy and chocolate to children on Easter morning.

INFERENCES

1) c
2) c

WORD POWER

1) a
2) b
3) a
4) c
5) a
6) b

CROSSWORD PUZZLE

ACROSS: 3) official 4) weather 6) crucifixion 7) rich 9) season 10) original 11) promise 12) decorate 13) sacred 16) symbols

DOWN: 1) goddess 2) Resurrection 5) worshippers 8) hare 14) rites 15) denial

Oktoberfest

1 A festival devoted to beer might be expected to be a particularly rowdy affair. A festival devoted to beer that lasts sixteen days could only be the world-famous wild party called Oktoberfest.

2 Oktoberfest, held annually in Munich, Germany, has been called the largest festival on earth, attracting more than seven million people from all over the world. The only object of the festival appears to be the consumption of German food and beer; Oktoberfest is also a celebration of German culture, both past and present.

3 The tradition of Oktoberfest goes back to the year 1810. On October seventeenth of that year, Bavarian Crown Prince Ludwig was married to Therese, the Princess of Saxony. The party celebrating the wedding lasted two days and attracted forty thousand people, at that time twice the population of Munich. Of course, beer was served, but there were also exhibitions of horse racing and marksmanship. The two-day party was held in a meadow, where a huge tent was erected. The popularity of the celebration led to the establishment of an annual event.

4 The site of Oktoberfest became known as the Theresienwiese, which means Therese Meadow, named in honor of Ludwig's bride. Oktoberfest festivities still take place at the same site, and run from the third weekend in September to the first weekend in October.

5   Oktoberfest begins when the first barrel, or keg, of beer is opened by the Lord Mayor of Munich. Throughout Oktoberfest, decorated brewery carts pulled by powerful horses clatter through the streets, piled with kegs of beer. The beer is served straight from the keg in large mugs called steins. The servers are dressed in traditional German costume.

6   The food served is traditional German fare, and amounts are appropriate for a huge feast. Whole oxen are turned on spits over open fires. There is fried chicken, pig's feet, sauerkraut and many different kinds of sausages.

7   On the second day of Oktoberfest, a huge parade travels the streets of Munich, to arrive finally at the Theresienwiese. The procession can be four miles long. The seven thousand participants are dressed in traditional costumes from all parts of Germany, and included are riflemen, folk dancers and brass bands.

8   Adding to the carnival atmosphere of Oktoberfest are the bright and colorful attractions and shows. Farmers attend an agricultural fair. Carousels, roller coasters and other rides are a constant source of light and noise, competing with the brass bands, many kinds of recorded music, and the crowds of people singing drinking songs and dancing.

9   Every seven years sees the performance of a traditional dance called the Cooper's Dance. A cooper is a person who makes the barrels which hold beer, and the Cooper's Dance is a custom with a five hundred year history. Dressed in the leather aprons of their occupation, twenty five coopers perform the traditional steps of the dance while beating on their barrels.

10   Oktoberfest is also celebrated in some cities in the United States and Canada, usually where there is a sizable community of people of German heritage. In Canada, the most popular Oktoberfest is held in Kitchener, Ontario, a place which until 1916 was known as Berlin.

MAIN IDEAS vs. SUPPORTING DETAILS

The following sentences are either Main Ideas or Supporting Details. Put an "M" beside those that are Main Ideas, and an "S" beside those that are Supporting Details.

1) _____ Oktoberfest has been called the largest festival on earth.
2) _____ Oktoberfest is a festival devoted to German beer, food and culture.
3) _____ The servers are dressed in traditional German costume.
4) _____ The traditional Cooper's Dance is performed every seven years.

UNDERSTANDING WHAT YOU READ

If you can, answer these questions from memory. If you cannot, look back at the article.

1) How was Bavarian Crown Prince Ludwig's wedding celebrated?

_____

2) What significance does Ludwig's wedding in 1810 have to the present-day Oktoberfest?

_____

3) How is beer served during Oktoberfest?

_____

4) What is the Cooper's Dance?

_____

REMEMBERING DETAILS

Write TRUE or FALSE under each statement. If the statement is false, write the statement correctly.

1) Oktoberfest is a festival solely devoted to beer.

_____

2) Bavarian Crown Prince Ludwig married the Princess of Saxony.

_____

3) The first barrel of beer for Oktoberfest is opened by a cooper.

_____

4) The dancers in the Cooper's Dance wear traditional German costume.

_____

INFERENCES

Based on the article, circle the letter of the best sentence completion.

1) Oktoberfest festivities still take place at the Theresienwiese because...

a) it is the only site in Munich big enough.
b) the tradition started there with Ludwig's wedding.
c) Therese became the Crown Princess of Germany.
d) there is space there for the horse-drawn brewery carts.

2) Oktoberfest is celebrated in other cities around the world because...

a) it is a famous festival.
b) everyone enjoys a wild party.
c) of the migration of Germans to other countries.
d) of the popularity of beer.

INTERPRETATION

1) How does Oktoberfest survive in today's climate of moderation? Discuss your ideas with a partner.

2) Would you find a feast composed of spit-roasted oxen, sausages, fried chicken, pig's feet and sauerkraut appetizing? What foods would you change? Write a menu for Oktoberfest based on your preferences.

3) Write a short composition explaining why you think the Cooper's Dance is only performed every seven years using twenty-five dancers.

WORD POWER

Circle the letter of the word that means the same as the word on the left.

1) wild	a) savage	b) boisterous	c) irresponsible
2) object	a) purpose	b) protest	c) thing
3) erected	a) raised	b) established	c) shaped
4) annual	a) yearly	b) festive	c) sporting
5) clatter	a) bicker	b) race	c) rattle
6) heritage	a) ancestry	b) inheritance	c) legacy

CROSSWORD PUZZLE

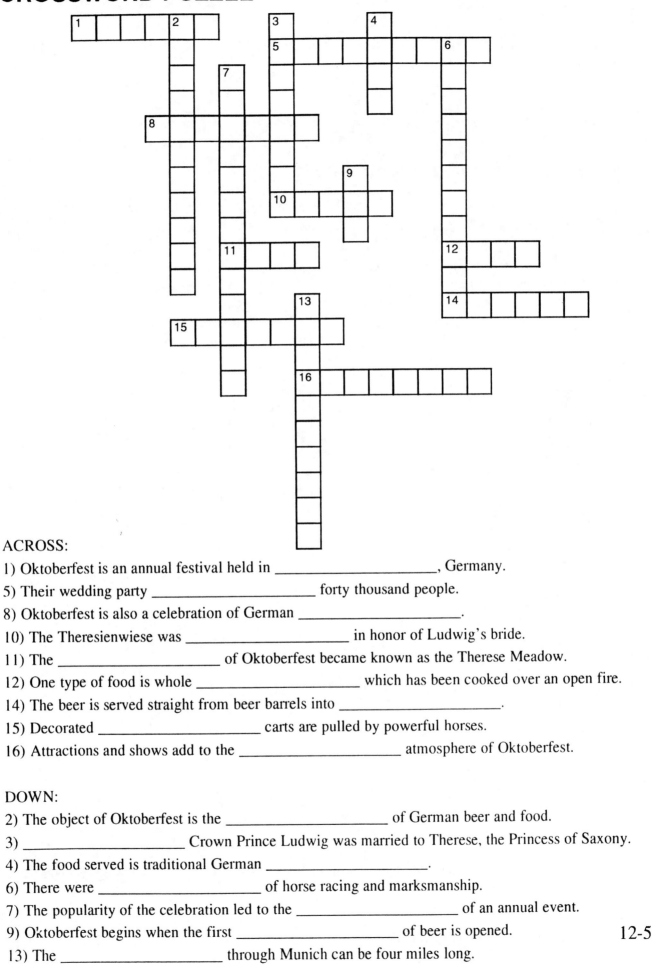

ACROSS:
1) Oktoberfest is an annual festival held in _____, Germany.
5) Their wedding party _____ forty thousand people.
8) Oktoberfest is also a celebration of German _____.
10) The Theresienwiese was _____ in honor of Ludwig's bride.
11) The _____ of Oktoberfest became known as the Therese Meadow.
12) One type of food is whole _____ which has been cooked over an open fire.
14) The beer is served straight from beer barrels into _____.
15) Decorated _____ carts are pulled by powerful horses.
16) Attractions and shows add to the _____ atmosphere of Oktoberfest.

DOWN:
2) The object of Oktoberfest is the _____ of German beer and food.
3) _____ Crown Prince Ludwig was married to Therese, the Princess of Saxony.
4) The food served is traditional German _____.
6) There were _____ of horse racing and marksmanship.
7) The popularity of the celebration led to the _____ of an annual event.
9) Oktoberfest begins when the first _____ of beer is opened.
13) The _____ through Munich can be four miles long.

12-5

ANSWER KEY

MAIN IDEAS vs SUPPORTING DETAILS

1) S
2) M
3) S
4) M

UNDERSTANDING WHAT YOU READ

1) Bavarian Crown Prince Ludwig's wedding was celebrated in a huge meadow and there was German beer and food, as well as exhibitions of horse racing and marksmanship.
2) The popularity of Ludwig's wedding led to the establishment of an annual event and Oktoberfest festivities still take place at the site of his wedding.
3) Beer is served by servers in traditional German costume from brewery carts pulled by powerful horses. The beer is served straight from the keg in large mugs called steins.
4) The Cooper's Dance is a traditional dance that is performed every seven years. Dressed in the leather aprons of their occupation, twenty-five coopers, people who make beer barrels, dance while beating on their beer barrels.

REMEMBERING DETAILS

1) F   Oktoberfest is a festival devoted to German beer, food and culture.
2) T
3) F   The first barrel of beer for Oktoberfest is opened by the Lord Mayor of Munich.
4) F   The dancers in the Cooper's Dance wear the leather aprons of their trade.

INFERENCES

1) b
2) c

WORD POWER

1) b
2) a
3) a
4) a
5) c
6) a

CROSSWORD PUZZLE

ACROSS: 1) Munich 5) attracted 8) culture 10) named 11) site 12) oxen 14) steins 15) brewery 16) carnival

DOWN: 2) consumption 3) Bavarian 4) fare 6) exhibitions 7) establishment 9) keg 13) procession

Earth Day

1   In the late 1770s, the Industrial Revolution marked the beginning of the modern age of machinery. With the rise of steam power and the invention of industrial machines and engines, mechanization began spreading from country to country and continent to continent. In families where generations had farmed the land for thousands of years, sons and daughters left home for new jobs with higher wages in factories in the city.

2   Although the new focus on industry helped many nations grow rich, the revolution has had a serious side effect: pollution. Through their smokestacks, factories around the world have pumped vast amounts of poisonous gas into the air. Industries have poured tons of toxic waste materials into freshwater streams, lakes and oceans. For many years scientists did not know what effects these things would have on humans and their environment.

3   Another problem was the growing focus on consumerism which led to a constant demand for new goods. Consumers buying new products were producing more garbage and waste than ever before. Also, much of the earth's natural forests were being chopped down to supply industries with materials, and animals were slowly being pushed out of their homes and their populations were being reduced. Mother Earth was quickly becoming a victim of industrial pollution and human neglect.

4   The 20th century has seen the beginning of a new revolution. Over

the first half of the century, people were becoming increasingly worried about the quality of their air, water and food. Others tried to focus attention on the increasing number of animals facing extinction. By the late 1960s groups of concerned people around the world were spending much of their time making others aware of the serious pollution problems facing the earth.

5   On April 22, 1970, the fight to save Mother Earth was given a much-needed boost when the United States declared Earth Day across the country. The day was given official government recognition in an attempt to draw public attention to the problem of air and water pollution. One of the major issues raised was the need to conserve the world's natural resources. The day is now considered the unofficial birthday of the modern environmental movement.

6   The first Earth Day turned out to be one of the largest mass demonstrations in the United States since the Second World War. Since that time, Earth Day has become an annual event across the U.S. and Canada. It is also observed in many other countries around the world.

7   In June 1992, the very first Earth Summit was held in Rio de Janeiro. It was all part of the new "green" movement that started with Earth Day. Over 100 heads of state and over 9,000 worldwide organizations attended the global conference on the environment. The goal was to develop a plan to help end the destruction of nature around the world.

8   Today people celebrate Earth Day in many different ways. Some plant trees and flowers, some groups organize cleaning crews to help pick up garbage, and others lobby the government to put an end to pollution.

9   By lending your hand on Earth Day, you are doing your part to ensure Mother Earth stays healthy for future generations.

MAIN IDEAS vs. SUPPORTING DETAILS

The following sentences are either Main Ideas or Supporting Details. Put an "M" beside those that are Main Ideas, and an "S" beside those that are Supporting Details.

1) _____ The Industrial Revolution began in the late 1770s.
2) _____ The new focus on industry resulted in pollution.
3) _____ People tried to focus attention on the growing number of animals facing extinction.
4) _____ Earth Day has become an annual event in many countries around the world.

13-2

UNDERSTANDING WHAT YOU READ

If you can, answer these questions from memory. If you cannot, look back at the article.

1) What marked the beginning of the modern age of machinery?

_____

2) How did consumerism create more pollution?

_____

3) How did the United States give the fight to save Mother Earth a boost?

_____

4) What was the meeting held in June, 1992 in Rio de Janeiro and what was its goal?

_____

REMEMBERING DETAILS

Write TRUE or FALSE under each statement. If the statement is false, write the statement correctly.

1) The Industrial Revolution made many people leave the city to take jobs on farms.

_____

2) The unofficial birthday of the modern environmental movement is April 22, 1970.

_____

3) Earth Day is only observed in the United States and Canada.

_____

4) Everyone celebrates Earth Day by lending a hand to clean up the environment.

_____

13-3

INFERENCES

Based on the article, circle the letter of the best sentence completion.

1) Mother Earth became a victim of industrial pollution and human neglect because...

a) of consumerism.
b) of the destruction of natural forests.
c) animals were being forced from their homes.
d) all of the above.

2) The United States gave the environmental movement a much needed boost because...

a) many U.S. citizens were moving out of the country due to the pollution problem.
b) groups of concerned people in the U.S. were lobbying for government support for their cause.
c) consumerism had grown out of control.
d) industry was putting pressure on the government.

INTERPRETATION

1) Industries are now required to follow rules when it comes to the handling of industrial waste. Write up your code of conduct for industries to follow when disposing of industrial waste.

2) Should endangered species be protected or should we follow a policy of "live and let live"?

3) What could you do to lend a hand on Earth Day? What do you think the government should do to help save the environment?

WORD POWER

Circle the letter of the word that means the same as the word on the left.

1) revolution	a) dramatic war	b) dramatic cycle	c) dramatic change
2) rise	a) breakthrough	b) ascent	c) addition
3) focus	a) sight	b) fixation	c) fascination
4) concerned	a) interested	b) affected	c) curious
5) heads of state	a) environmentalists	b) lobbyists	c) world leaders
6) lobby	a) persuade	b) get	c) foyer

13-4

CROSSWORD PUZZLE

ACROSS:
2) Mother Earth was becoming a victim of industrial _____.
4) Industries began pouring tons of _____ waste materials into the water.
6) Earth Day is considered the unofficial birthday of the modern _____ movement.
8) Vast amounts of _____ gas was pumped into the air.
11) One of the issues raised was the need to _____ the world's natural resources.
12) _____ of farmers had farmed the land for thousands of years.
13) The new focus on _____ helped many nations grow rich.
14) The Industrial Revolution _____ the beginning of the modern age of machinery.
15) We should all help on Earth Day by _____ a hand.

DOWN:
1) The Earth Summit, in June, 1992 was a _____ conference on the environment.
3) Much of the earth's _____ forests were being chopped down.
5) The growing focus on _____ was another problem.
6) There were an increasing number of animals facing _____.
7) Earth Day is _____ in many countries around the world.
9) A _____ was given to the fight to save Mother Earth by the United States.
10) The United States _____ Earth Day across the country.

ANSWER KEY

MAIN IDEAS vs SUPPORTING DETAILS

1) S
2) M
3) S
4) M

UNDERSTANDING WHAT YOU READ

1) The Industrial Revolution, with the rise of steam power and the invention of industrial machines and engines, marked the beginning of the modern age of machinery.
2) Consumerism and the constant demand for new goods created more pollution because it led to the production of more garbage and waste.
3) The United States gave the fight to save Mother Earth a boost by declaring Earth Day on April 22, 1970.
4) In June, 1992 the first Earth Summit was held in Rio de Janeiro and its goal was to develop a plan to help end the destruction of nature around the world.

REMEMBERING DETAILS

1) F   The Industrial Revolution made many people leave the farms to take jobs in the city.
2) T
3) F   Earth Day is an annual event in the United States and Canada, but it is also observed in many other countries around the world.
4) F   Everyone celebrates Earth Day in different ways. Some plant trees and flowers, some organize cleaning crews and others lobby the government to put an end to pollution.

INFERENCES

1) d
2) b

WORD POWER

1) c
2) a
3) b
4) a
5) c
6) a

CROSSWORD PUZZLE

ACROSS: 2) pollution 4) toxic 6) environmental 8) poisonous 11) conserve 12) generations 13) industry 14) marked 15) lending

DOWN: 1) global 3) natural 5) consumerism 6) extinction 7) observed 9) boost 10) declared

Confucius' Birthday or Teacher's Day

1   The quality of a person's thoughts can be measured by the endurance of those thoughts through the ages. When one person's thoughts endure for twenty-five centuries, that person obviously has much to teach us all.

2   The Chinese philosopher Confucius was born in the year 551 BC, and throughout his life he taught a system of ethics that now bear the name Confucianism. Confucius' ethics were based on selflessness, respect and the importance of the family as a social unit. His most famous teaching, known as the "Golden Rule," is familiar to people all over the world: "Do not do unto others what you would not want others to do unto you."

3   Though denounced as spiritualism in Communist China, Confucianism has continued as an important aspect of life in the Far East. One way Confucius has remained an important figure is through the celebration of his birthday.

4   The site of Confucius' birth is found in a town in northeast China called Qufu. In Qufu, Confucius' birthday is celebrated over a two week period in September and October. The celebration is known as the Confucian Culture Festival, and is headquartered in a palace built by Confucius' descendants both as their home and as the center of the Confucian philosophy. Many of the people of Qufu still consider themselves to be direct descendants of Confucius.

5   The festivities in Qufu serve two purposes: one is a celebration of

Confucius' life and thoughts, the other is an example to the Chinese people of the endurance of Confucius' ideals despite Communist disapproval.

6   The whole town takes part in the festivities, filling the streets and forming a great procession on the avenue leading to the palace. Children carry flowers and colorful banners and they dance. Bands play the ancient music of drums, gongs, flutes and trumpets. Girls wear masks of cats or monkeys, and they ride horses made of papier-mâché. Colorful paper dragons dance and weave along the avenue. Firecrackers explode all along the way, and at the palace walls.

7   The festival at Qufu is also attended by Confucian scholars from all over China. With them the celebration of Confucius' birthday takes a more serious tone with lectures and exhibitions on Confucius' life and philosophy, and on Chinese customs.

8   Other countries besides China celebrate the birth of Confucius. Korea, Japan and Taiwan have also been influenced by Confucius' teaching.

9   In Taiwan, the day of Confucius' birth is a national holiday honoring teachers. Teacher's Day, as the holiday is known, is an expression of one of Confucianism's central teachings: the close bond to be held between teacher and student. The student-teacher relationship is considered as a variation on the relationship between children and their ancestors, and is important as a way to perpetuate traditional values from generation to generation.

10   In South Korea, celebrations take place at a Confucian shrine in the city of Seoul. Music and dance of many years past are performed. Men dressed in traditional scarlet robes recreate ancient dance steps to the music of flutes.

11   The continued celebration of the life of Confucius is vital in maintaining the existence of Confucius' philosophy, and is an important reminder of the virtues found in his teachings.

MAIN IDEAS vs. SUPPORTING DETAILS

The following sentences are either Main Ideas or Supporting Details. Put an "M" beside those that are Main Ideas, and an "S" beside those that are Supporting Details.

1) _____ Confucianism was denounced as spiritualism in Communist China.
2) _____ Confucianism has remained an important aspect of life in the Far East.
3) _____ The Confucian Culture Festival is celebrated in Qufu over a two week period.
4) _____ The festival at Qufu is also attended by Confucian scholars from all over China.

UNDERSTANDING WHAT YOU READ

If you can, answer these questions from memory. If you cannot, look back at the article.

1) On what were Confucius' ethics based?

___

2) Who considers themselves direct descendants of Confucius?

___

3) What countries celebrate Confucius' birthday?

___

4) In what country is Confucius' birthday known as Teacher's Day?

___

REMEMBERING DETAILS

Write TRUE or FALSE under each statement. If the statement is false, write the statement correctly.

1) Confucius' most famous teaching is "Do not do unto others what you would have them do unto you."

___

2) The Communists embraced Confucius' teachings.

___

3) The celebration in Qufu is headquartered in a local school.

___

4) One of Confucianism's central teachings is the close bond held between student and teacher.

___

14-3

INFERENCES

Based on the article, circle the letter of the best sentence completion.

1) Confucius' thoughts have endured for twenty-five centuries because...

a) he was born in 551 BC.
b) of their quality.
c) of the popularity of his "Golden Rule."
d) of the celebrations for his birthday.

2) The town of Qufu is the center of the Confucian Culture Festival because...

a) Confucian scholars from all over China attend the festival.
b) of the great procession that leads to the palace.
c) of the palace built there by Confucius' descendants.
d) it is the place of Confucius' birth.

INTERPRETATION

1) Has Confucius' "Golden Rule" been adopted worldwide as a guiding principle? If not, do you think it should be?

2) Do you think that Confucius' teachings are examples of spiritualism? Discuss.

3) Write a short composition naming the greatest teacher in your life and what that person taught you.

WORD POWER

Circle the letter of the word that means the same as the word on the left.

1) system	a) examination	b) order	c) theory
2) ideals	a) concepts	b) models	c) testimonies
3) despite	a) contrary to	b) contempt for	c) not spiteful
4) influenced	a) rejoiced	b) argued	c) affected
5) central	a) moderate	b) principle	c) infamous
6) variation	a) regulation	b) modification	c) lessening

CROSSWORD PUZZLE

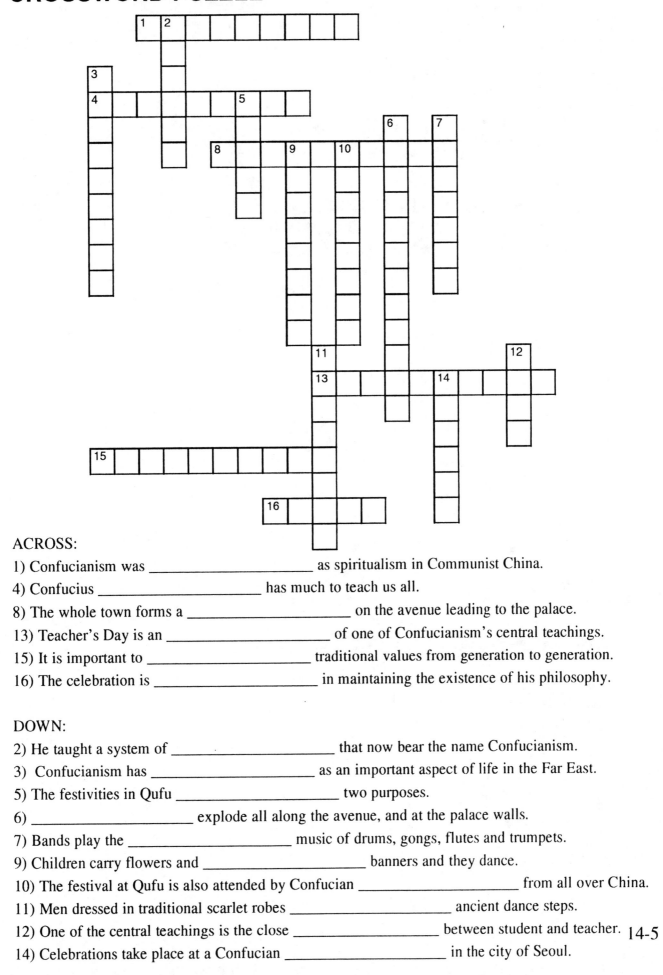

ACROSS:

1) Confucianism was _____ as spiritualism in Communist China.
4) Confucius _____ has much to teach us all.
8) The whole town forms a _____ on the avenue leading to the palace.
13) Teacher's Day is an _____ of one of Confucianism's central teachings.
15) It is important to _____ traditional values from generation to generation.
16) The celebration is _____ in maintaining the existence of his philosophy.

DOWN:

2) He taught a system of _____ that now bear the name Confucianism.
3) Confucianism has _____ as an important aspect of life in the Far East.
5) The festivities in Qufu _____ two purposes.
6) _____ explode all along the avenue, and at the palace walls.
7) Bands play the _____ music of drums, gongs, flutes and trumpets.
9) Children carry flowers and _____ banners and they dance.
10) The festival at Qufu is also attended by Confucian _____ from all over China.
11) Men dressed in traditional scarlet robes _____ ancient dance steps.
12) One of the central teachings is the close _____ between student and teacher.
14) Celebrations take place at a Confucian _____ in the city of Seoul.

14-5

ANSWER KEY

MAIN IDEA vs SUPPORTING DETAILS

1) S
2) M
3) M
4) S

UNDERSTANDING WHAT YOU READ

1) Confucius' ethics were based on selflessness, respect and the importance of the family as a social unit.
2) Many of the people of Qufu consider themselves to be direct descendants of Confucius.
3) China, Korea, Japan and Taiwan celebrate Confucius' birthday.
4) In Taiwan, the day of Confucius' birth is a national holiday honoring teachers. That day is known as Teacher's Day.

REMEMBERING DETAILS

1) F   Confucius' most famous teaching is "Do not do unto others what you would not want others to do unto you."
2) F   Confucius' teachings were denounced as spiritualism in Communist China.
3) F   The celebration in Qufu is headquartered in a palace built by Confucius' descendants.
4) T

INFERENCES

1) b
2) d

WORD POWER

1) c
2) a
3) a
4) c
5) b
6) b

CROSSWORD PUZZLE

ACROSS: 1) denounced 4) obviously 8) procession 13) expression 15) perpetuate 16) vital

DOWN: 2) ethics 3) continued 5) serve 6) firecrackers 7) ancient 9) colorful 10) scholars 11) recreate 12) bond 14) shrine

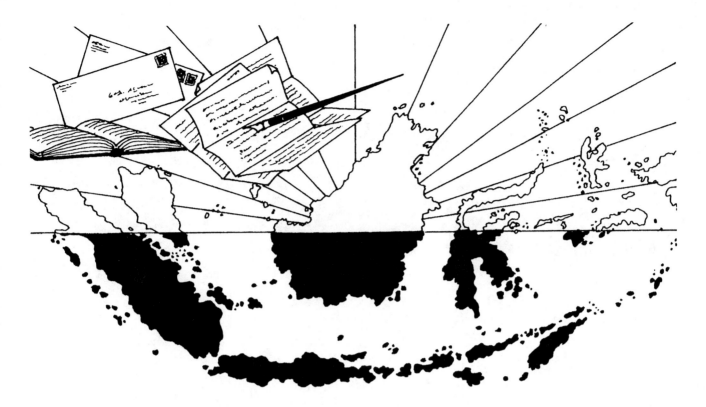

Kartini Day

1   After China, India and the United States, Indonesia is the world's most populated country. It is also the only one of its size spread over a vast archipelago, a geographical term for a chain or group of many islands. In fact, if you were to visit one Indonesian island every day, it would take you nearly 48 years to visit them all.

2   The Indonesian national motto "Unity through Diversity" helps explain how a nation of people spread across more than 17,000 islands can remain so closely united. But even though great distances separate the Indonesian people, they share a fierce pride in their country and their national heroes. Of all the Indonesian heroes, perhaps the most celebrated female is Raden Ajeng Kartini.

3   On April 21st each year, Indonesians celebrate Kartini Day in honor of her birth. She was born in 1879, the daughter of a noble Indonesian family. It was not until after her death, however, that her name became associated with the Indonesian women's movement and the entire country's struggle for independence.

4   As a nation, Indonesia has been fighting for its independence for centuries. This diverse land of tropical rain forests, jungle wetlands, snow-covered mountains and beautiful beaches has attracted the interests of many different countries. Portugal, Spain, Holland, Britain and Japan have all taken advantage of Indonesian resources for their own profit.

5   It was the Dutch, however, who gained lasting influence in Indonesia. Although they helped modernize many of the islands and provided education to privileged Indonesians, the Dutch became masters of the land and its people. Under Dutch rule, many Indonesians farmers were forced to raise crops that were sent directly to Holland. Over the years, many battles broke out between Dutch colonists and native Indonesians yearning for independence.

6   Women played a large role in the struggle for freedom from Dutch rule. However, many Indonesian women were also critical of the way they were treated by their own countrymen, who put severe limits on their freedom and denied them their right to an education.

7   As a princess who attended a Dutch school, Lady Kartini was exposed to many Western ideas on the treatment of women. After leaving the school, she remained in close contact with her Dutch friends through a series of letters. In her letters she expressed concern for the women of Indonesia, criticized the restrictions placed on them by their fellow countrymen, and detailed the loss of basic rights suffered by all Indonesians under colonial rule.

8   After marrying in 1903, Lady Kartini became more active in her fight to gain equal rights for women. Her influence spread across Indonesia and inspired many other women to take up the cause. In 1904, Kartini died while giving birth at the young age of 24. In 1910, her letters were published under the title "Through Darkness into Light." They helped bring the problems of Indonesian women to the attention of the world and created the support for the Kartini Foundation.

9   The Kartini Foundation worked diligently to free Indonesia from the Dutch and to give women equal rights to education and voting. In 1916, the Kartini Foundation opened the first girl's school in Java. Today on Kartini Day, Indonesian women dress in their national colors to symbolize the freedom gained through the efforts of Raden Ajeng Kartini.

MAIN IDEAS vs. SUPPORTING DETAILS

The following sentences are either Main Ideas or Supporting Details. Put an "M" beside those that are Main Ideas, and an "S" beside those that are Supporting Details.

1) _____ Indonesia is the only country of its size spread over a vast archipelago.
2) _____ The Indonesian motto is "Unity through Diversity."
3) _____ The Dutch gained lasting influence in Indonesia.
4) _____ Lady Kartini's letters helped bring the problems of Indonesian women to the attention of the world.

UNDERSTANDING WHAT YOU READ

If you can, answer these questions from memory. If you cannot, look back at the article.

1) How long would it take you to visit every island of Indonesia?

_____

2) What do all Indonesians share?

_____

3) Which countries have taken advantage of Indonesia's rich natural and human resources?

_____

4) How did Indonesian men treat their women?

_____

REMEMBERING DETAILS

Write TRUE or FALSE under each statement. If the statement is false, write the statement correctly.

1) An archipelago is a vast nation surrounded by water.

_____

2) The most celebrated female Indonesian hero is Lady Kartini.

_____

3) Raden Ajeng Kartini was born into a family of Indonesian farmers.

_____

4) Lady Kartini campaigned exclusively for the rights of Indonesian women.

_____

INFERENCES

Based on the article, circle the letter of the best sentence completion.

1) Battles broke out between Dutch colonists and native Indonesians because...

a) the Indonesians would not turn over all their crops.
b) the Indonesians resented Dutch rule.
c) the Dutch only provided education to privileged Indonesians.
d) the Dutch put severe limits on women's freedom.

2) Lady Kartini fought to gain equal rights for Indonesian women because...

a) she was born to a noble family.
b) as a princess she had attended a Dutch school
c) of the views expressed to her in letters from her Dutch friends.
d) after attending a Dutch school, she felt Westerners treated their women more fairly.

INTERPRETATION

1) What type of personal motto would you use? Share your motto, and its explanation, with your class.

2) Do you have a personal hero? Write a short composition describing your hero.

3) Is there a cause you support? Write a short paragraph about your cause.

WORD POWER

Circle the letter of the word that means the same as the word on the left.

1) diversity	a) deviation	b) aversion	c) variety
2) united	a) connected	b) married	c) related
3) fierce	a) desperate	b) intense	c) violent
4) resources	a) assets	b) properties	c) resorts
5) yearning	a) asking	b) longing	c) resorts
6) exposed	a) naked	b) endangered	c) subjected

CROSSWORD PUZZLE

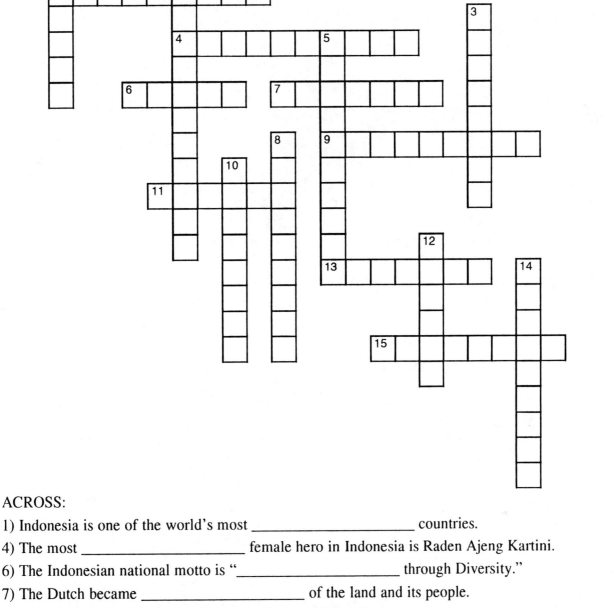

ACROSS:
1) Indonesia is one of the world's most _____ countries.
4) The most _____ female hero in Indonesia is Raden Ajeng Kartini.
6) The Indonesian national motto is "_____ through Diversity."
7) The Dutch became _____ of the land and its people.
9) Indonesia has been fighting for its own independence for _____.
11) The Dutch _____ lasting influence in Indonesia.
13) Indonesia is a _____ land that has attracted the interests of many countries.
15) Many Indonesian women were _____ of the way they were treated.

DOWN:
1) Indonesian people share a fierce _____ in their country and their national heroes.
2) Indonesia is spread out over a vast _____.
3) She detailed the loss of basic rights suffered by all Indonesians under _____ rule.
5) Kartini's name became _____ with the struggle for equality and independence.
8) The Dutch helped _____ many of the islands.
10) Lady Kartini _____ many other women to take up the cause.
12) Many countries have used Indonesian resources for their own _____.
14) She was exposed to many Western ideas on the _____ of women.

ANSWER KEY

MAIN IDEAS vs SUPPORTING DETAILS

1) S
2) S
3) M
4) M

UNDERSTANDING WHAT YOU READ

1) It would take you nearly 48 years to visit every Indonesian island.
2) All Indonesians share a fierce pride in their country and their national heroes.
3) Portugal, Spain, Holland, Britain and Japan have all taken advantage of Indonesia's rich natural and human resources.
4) Indonesian men put severe limits on the freedoms offered to women and denied them their right to an education.

REMEMBERING DETAILS

1) F   An archipelago is a geographical term for a chain or group of many islands.
2) T
3) F   Raden Ajeng Kartini was born into a noble Indonesian family.
4) F   In addition to campaigning for the rights of Indonesian women, Lady Kartini also wrote letters detailing the loss of basic rights suffered by all Indonesians under colonial rule.

INFERENCES

1) b
2) d

WORD POWER

1) c
2) a
3) b
4) a
5) b
6) c

CROSSWORD PUZZLE

ACROSS: 1) populated 4) celebrated 6) Unity 7) masters 9) centuries 11) gained 13) diverse 15) critical

DOWN: 1) pride 2) archipelago 3) colonial 5) associated 8) modernize 10) inspired 12) profit 14) treatment

Kupalo Festival

1   The Kupalo Festival is filled with the magic and mystery of the ages. It takes place when the natural world is in the full glory of the summer. Years ago, time for the Kupalo Festival also meant time for a visit from a character from the supernatural world.

2   Taking place in the Ukraine, the Kupalo Festival today is a midsummer celebration of the coming harvest. The festival occurs on June 24, just as the days begin to shorten toward autumn.

3   The origin of the festival goes back to a time before Christ, when nature and the seasons were surrounded by a mythology of magical gods and creatures. Traditionally, the middle of the summer is believed to be the time of year when the earth reveals its secrets, when trees speak, and supernatural creatures like witches and vampires are present.

4   The figure of Kupalo comes from this pagan belief. Kupalo was the god of the harvest, as well as the god of love and of the fertility of the earth. The legend of Kupalo is that he would appear in the spring, after sleeping under a tree all winter, and he would shake the tree so vigorously that the seeds would fall to the ground. This appearance by Kupalo served as a sign of how abundant that year's harvest would be.

5   The Kupalo festivities would take place outside of villages and towns, usually in a forest or near a river or a pond. Those celebrating the Kupalo

Festival were mainly young unmarried men and young unmarried women.

6   During the festival, the participants would decorate a small tree with flowers, herbs, seeds and fruit; the tree was meant to represent the god Kupalo. The young people would perform a ritual dance around the Kupalo figure. Then, to symbolize the decline in the earth's fertility from this day on, this "scarecrow" was torn apart and spread onto the fields.

7   But the Kupalo festival was also a celebration of love, and a time when young women would try to attract young men in hopes of marriage. For this reason the young women would dress themselves in garlands of herbs and flowers. One young women would be chosen as the most beautiful. She would then stand in the center of a circle of her friends, who would dance around her as she distributed to certain young women amongst them the flowers and wreaths they would wear. The wreaths had special significance: the young ladies who received a wreath were believed to be the ones who would marry that year.

8   The young people would all celebrate together at the culmination of the Kupalo Festival. In a custom dating back to the festival's pagan origins, a bonfire would be lit, and the festival participants would dance hand in hand around it, singing ritual songs. The fire would be fed with herbs and items no longer needed. As the celebration would progress, the young people would leap over the fire as it burned. The fire would never be extinguished, but would be allowed to burn out.

9   Sadly, today much of the magic of the Kupalo celebration is gone, and the festival is observed primarily as a harvest festival, without its theme of love. However, the strength of the Ukrainian culture can be seen in the continued existence of the Kupalo Festival over many centuries.

MAIN IDEAS vs. SUPPORTING DETAILS

The following sentences are either Main Ideas or Supporting Details. Put an "M" beside those that are Main Ideas, and an "S" beside those that are Supporting Details.

1) _____ On June 24, the days begin to shorten toward autumn.
2) _____ The Kupalo Festival dates back to a time before Christ.
3) _____ Kupalo was the god of the harvest, as well as the god of the fertility of the earth.
4) _____ During the Kupalo Festival, young women would dress themselves in garlands of herbs and flowers.

UNDERSTANDING WHAT YOU READ

If you can, answer these questions from memory. If you cannot, look back at the article.

1) What is the Kupalo Festival?

_____

2) Who was Kupalo?

_____

3) What did the "scarecrow" symbolize?

_____

4) How was the end of the Kupalo Festival celebrated?

_____

REMEMBERING DETAILS

Write TRUE or FALSE under each statement. If the statement is false, write the statement correctly.

1) The Kupalo Festival takes place in early autumn.

_____

2) Kupalo appears in midsummer after sleeping under the ground.

_____

3) Young men and women would celebrate the culmination of the Kupalo Festival separately.

_____

4) Today the Kupalo Festival is primarily a harvest festival, without its theme of love.

_____

16-3

INFERENCES

Based on the article, circle the letter of the best sentence completion.

1) The Kupalo Festival is celebrated on June 24 because...

a) it is the first day of autumn.
b) it is when the earth's fertility starts to decline toward autumn.
c) it is the beginning of the harvest season.
d) it is the first day of summer.

2) The Kupalo Festival is mainly celebrated by young unmarried men and women because...

a) they are on summer vacation from school at that time.
b) all the older men and women must work.
c) of the strenuous physical activities involved.
d) it is a time when young women try to attract young men in the hopes of marriage.

INTERPRETATION

1) Discuss with a partner reasons why a pagan festival, like the Kupalo Festival, has survived for over two thousand years.

2) Write a short composition describing the symbolism in the use of a tree to represent the Kupalo figure.

3) Lights and fires are important parts of many celebrations. With a partner, make a list comparing the symbolic and traditional uses of light and fire in different holidays and festivals you know about.

WORD POWER

Circle the letter of the word that means the same as the word on the left.

1) glory	a) splendor	b) honor	c) distinction
2) pagan	a) peaceful	b) heathen	c) earthen
3) abundant	a) bountiful	b) opulent	c) scarce
4) decline	a) slope	b) jump	c) decrease
5) garlands	a) clothes	b) wreaths	c) hats
6) extinguished	a) put out	b) destroyed	c) obscured

16-4

CROSSWORD PUZZLE

ACROSS:
1) The Kupalo Festival is filled with the magic and _____ of the ages.
2) The festival occurs just as the days begin to shorten toward _____.
5) The fire was fed with _____ and items no longer needed.
6) One young women would distribute _____ to certain other young ladies.
8) The figure of Kupalo comes form this pagan _____.
10) They believed the young women who received wreaths would _____ that year.
13) The Kupalo _____ took place outside of villages and towns.
14) Today much of the _____ of the Kupalo celebration is gone.

DOWN:
1) The Kupalo Festival is a _____ celebration of the coming harvest.
3) There is a _____ surrounding the origins of the festival.
4) During the festival the _____ would decorate a small tree.
7) The festival is observed primarily as a harvest festival without its _____ of love.
8) The fire would never be extinguished, but it would be allowed to _____ out.
9) Kupalo was also the god of the _____ of the earth.
11) The lighting of a bonfire is a _____ dating back to pagan times.
12) The young people would _____ over the fire as it burned.

16-5

ANSWER KEY

MAIN IDEAS vs SUPPORTING DETAILS

1) S
2) M
3) M
4) S

UNDERSTANDING WHAT YOU READ

1) The Kupalo Festival is a midsummer celebration of the coming harvest which also used to incorporate supernatural beliefs.
2) Kupalo was the god of the harvest, as well as the god of love and of the fertility of the earth.
3) The "scarecrow" symbolized the god Kupalo.
4) At the end of the Kupalo Festival the young people would celebrate together near a bonfire. They would dance, sing and leap over this bonfire, which would be allowed to burn out rather than being extinguished.

REMEMBERING DETAILS

1) F   The Kupalo Festival takes place on June 24, just as the days begin to shorten toward autumn.
2) F   Kupalo appears in the spring after sleeping under a tree.
3) F   Young men and women celebrate together at the culmination of the Kupalo Festival.
4) T

INFERENCES

1) b
2) d

WORD POWER

1) a
2) b
3) a
4) c
5) b
6) a

CROSSWORD PUZZLE

ACROSS: 1) mystery 2) autumn 5) herbs 6) wreaths 8) belief 10) marry 13) festivities 14) magic

DOWN: 1) midsummer 3) mythology 4) participants 7) theme 8) burn 9) fertility 11) custom 12) leap

Zulu Festival

1   The Zulu tribe of Southern Africa existed long before the arrival of the first white settler. However, European missionaries brought their Christianity to the Zulus, and though the proud tribe has maintained many aspects of its own culture, it has also been influenced by the Christian religion. This blend of cultures is given fascinating display in the festivals of the Nazareth Baptist Church.

2   The Nazareth Baptist Church was founded by Isaiah Shembe in 1911. While heavily influenced by Western Christianity and the Old Testament of the Bible, it has also kept elements of the ancient beliefs of the Zulu people.

3   There are three annual festivals amongst Shembe's sect, but the Zulu Festival held in July is the most popular. The festival is also known as the Shembe Festival, and the unique form of the festival's celebrations follows directions Shembe himself received through voices he heard.

4   The Zulu Festival lasts an entire month: it begins on the first day of July and continues to the last Sunday of the month. There are an estimated five hundred thousand members of the Shembe's Baptist sect, and the festival draws as many as 20,000 members from all over South Africa and neighboring countries. Some people will stay for the entire month, living in temporary encampments.

5   The main activity of the festival is a traditional form of dancing, but the

days of dancing must alternate with days of rest. Following Biblical teaching, Saturday is always a day of rest and prayer, but on Sunday the dancing and festivities resume. Sundays are the most widely attended days of the festival.

6   During the festival, time is also devoted to the preaching of sermons, speeches by church members and prayers for the sick.

7   One peculiar feature of the festival is the separation of the men and women throughout the month. Living quarters are segregated, with one area reserved for tribal chiefs, one area for the married men and their sons, and areas for both the married and unmarried women. Even the festive dancing is performed under these strict rules of separation; each group dances in a particular area. In addition, young men dance in their own group, while older men wear traditional dress and dance amongst themselves.

8   The most colorful day of the festival is the final one, and this is the most popular day for both participants and spectators. On the last Sunday of July the dancing can last all day long; this is made possible by the unique manner in which the dancers participate.

9   The dance takes place in a large field. On one side of the field are the spectators. Facing them is a row of dancers in traditional Zulu costume; this row can stretch to include fifty people. Behind each dancer in the row is a long line of dancers, and slowly the dancers move from the back of the line to take their place at the front. In this way a dancer, by gradually being shifted to the back of the line, can rest or leave the group altogether.

10   The importance of the Zulu Festival can be seen in the way it preserves the many traditions which give the Nazareth Baptist Church its unique identity. We can only assume that Isaiah Shembe's "voices" had this preservation in mind.

MAIN IDEAS vs. SUPPORTING DETAILS

The following sentences are either Main Ideas or Supporting Details. Put an "M" beside those that are Main Ideas, and an "S" beside those that are Supporting Details.

1) _____ The Zulu Festival is the most popular of the Shembe sect's three annual festivals.
2) _____ The Nazareth Baptist Church was founded by Isaiah Shembe in 1911.
3) _____ Men and women are separated during the Zulu Festival.
4) _____ The most colorful and popular day of the festival is the final one.

UNDERSTANDING WHAT YOU READ

If you can, answer these questions from memory. If you cannot, look back at the article.

1) What were the influences on the Nazareth Baptist Church?

___

2) When is the Zulu Festival held?

___

3) What is the most popular day of the entire Zulu Festival?

___

4) How long does the dancing last on the final day of the festival? How is this achieved?

___

REMEMBERING DETAILS

Write TRUE or FALSE under each statement. If the statement is false, write the statement correctly.

1) The unique form of the Zulu Festival's celebrations is due to the influence of Western Christianity.

___

2) An estimated five hundred thousand people attend the annual Zulu Festival.

___

3) Some of the festival's activities are the preaching of sermons, speeches by church members and prayers for the sick.

___

4) On the final day of the festival, dancers must be prepared to dance for the entire day.

___

17-3

INFERENCES

Based on the article, circle the letter of the best sentence completion.

1) The Zulu Festival is also known as the Shembe Festival because...

a) Shembe founded the Nazareth Baptist Church.
b) the festival's celebrations follow directions Shembe received through voices.
c) the Zulus wanted to honor Shembe for his work with the Baptist church.
d) the Baptist church wanted to honor Shembe for his work with the Zulu tribe.

2) The final day of dancing takes place in a large field because...

a) it is the traditional field used for the festival.
b) it is the place of Shembe's death.
c) of its proximity to the temporary encampments of visiting church members.
d) of the large number of participants.

INTERPRETATION

1) Why do you think that Shembe insisted that days of rest were to follow days of dancing? Brainstorm possible reasons with a partner.

2) An interesting feature of the festival is the separation of the men and women. Write a short composition describing what you think Shembe's reasons were for this concept.

3) Based on the story of the Zulu Festival, what are some of the traditions which give the Baptist sect its identity? Make a list and then compare your list with that of a partner.

WORD POWER

Circle the letter of the word that means the same as the word on the left.

1) blend	a) unity	b) mix	c) singularity
2) elements	a) features	b) compounds	c) weather
3) temporary	a) subtle	b) alternate	c) not permanent
4) resume	a) summary	b) continue	c) discontinue
5) strict	a) rigid	b) lax	c) religious
6) unique	a) unusual	b) solitary	c) necessary

CROSSWORD PUZZLE

ACROSS:

2) The Zulu tribe _____ long before the arrival of the first white settler.
3) One peculiar feature of the festival is the _____ of the men and women.
4) The Zulu Festival is the most _____ of the three annual festivals.
5) The directions for the festival came to Shembe through voices he _____.
7) The most colorful day of the festival is the _____ one.
9) Some people stay for the entire month and live in temporary _____.
12) The row of dancers can _____ to include fifty people.
14) Older men wear traditional dress and dance _____ themselves.
15) On the last Sunday of July the _____ participate in a unique manner.
16) The Zulu Festival _____ many Zulu traditions.

DOWN:

1) European _____ brought their Christianity to the Zulus.
6) Sundays are the most _____ attended days of the Zulu Festival.
8) On one side of the field are the _____.
10) The days of dancing must _____ with days of rest.
11) Living quarters for the festival are _____.
13) After shifting to the back of the _____, a dancer can rest or leave.

17-5

ANSWER KEY

MAIN IDEAS vs SUPPORTING DETAILS

1) M
2) S
3) M
4) M

UNDERSTANDING WHAT YOU READ

1) The influences on The Nazareth Baptist Church were Western Christianity, the Old Testament of the Bible and ancient beliefs of the Zulu people.
2) The Zulu Festival lasts an entire month: it begins on the first day of July and continues to the last Sunday of the month.
3) The most popular day of the entire Zulu Festival is the final one, the last Sunday in July.
4) On the last day of the Zulu Festival the dancing can last all day. This is due to the Zulu's unique style of dancing. The Zulu's have perfected a style of dancing that features continuous dancing, while allowing individual dancers opportunities to rest or leave the group altogether.

REMEMBERING DETAILS

1) F   The unique form of the Zulu Festival's celebrations follows directions Shembe received through voices he heard.
2) F   As many as 20,000 people attend the annual Zulu Festival. There are an estimated five hundred thousand members of the Shembe's Baptist sect.
3) T
4) F   On the final day of the festival, dancers can rest or leave the group of dancers as others take their place in front of the spectators.

INFERENCES

1) b
2) d

WORD POWER

1) b
2) a
3) c
4) b
5) a
6) a

CROSSWORD PUZZLE

ACROSS: 2) existed 3) separation 4) popular 5) heard 7) final 9) encampments 12) stretch 14) amongst 15) dancers 16) preserves

DOWN: 1) missionaries 6) widely 8) spectators 10) alternate 11) segregated 13) line

Songkran

1   Thailand has been called the Land of Elephants and the Land of Enchantment. When translated, its modern name, Muang Thai, means Land of the Free. But perhaps the most fitting nickname is Land of the Smiles, and judging by the quality of life in Thailand it is easy to see why.

2   Thailand is one of the most modern and wealthy nations in Southeast Asia. Despite being located 125 kilometers (75 miles) south of China, the world's most populated nation, Thailand remains the only country in Southeast Asia that has never been conquered and colonized by another country.

3   That could be one reason why the people of Thailand are some of the proudest, friendliest people in the world. Life in this tropical nation, once known as Siam, is very good. With its year-round warm weather, abundant rice fields and large Buddhist community, Thailand offers its citizens a safe, stable and prosperous place in which to live.

4   It is also a nation of citizens that like to enjoy themselves. Throughout the year, the people of Thailand celebrate dozens of regional and national festivals. Some hold important religious meanings, while others are held just for the fun of it. These include the Visakha Puga (celebrating the birth of Buddha), the Boon Bong Fai or Rocket Festival, the Flower Festival, Chakri Day and Loy Krathong, a beautiful three-day event where waterways in Thailand are lit up

with millions of candles.

5   One of the biggest national celebrations in Thailand is known as Songkran. This is held every April thirteenth to celebrate traditional New Year in Thailand. The entire Songkran festival takes place over a three day period, from April twelfth to the fourteenth, and it includes many different religious and public activities. Young and old alike participate in Songkran rituals, many of which involve showering each other with water.

6   In Thailand's many Buddhist temples, water is sprinkled on Buddhist images during Songkran. This is done to symbolize the cleansing of the spirit, and Kings often take a ceremonial bath to honor Buddha. Elder citizens of Thailand also have water sprinkled on their hands and feet by the young in a traditional show of respect.

7   In the capital city of Bangkok, festival highlights include giant parades, with beautifully-decorated floats and marching bands playing a variety of Eastern instruments. In some areas, large groups of Buddhist monks gather to receive gifts from local citizens. Vendors can be found selling caged birds and live fish, which are bought and released in the belief that doing so will bring good luck.

8   In Chiang Mai in northern Thailand, the festival is taken into the streets, where crowds of people dance and watch beauty contests to celebrate Songkran. Throughout the festival, there is a great deal of water-splashing all across Thailand, especially among young people. Splashing water on another person during Songkran is a way of offering them your blessings and wishes for happiness and good health. The more water that gets splashed, the more blessing a person will receive.

9   With all these blessings, it is easy to find smiles on the faces of people all across Thailand. Songkran is certainly one time when the country lives up to its most fitting nickname.

MAIN IDEAS vs. SUPPORTING DETAILS

The following sentences are either Main Ideas or Supporting Details. Put an "M" beside those that are Main Ideas, and an "S" beside those that are Supporting Details.

1) _____ Thailand's modern name is Muang Thai, which means Land of the Free.
2) _____ The quality of life in Thailand is very good.
3) _____ Songkran is one of Thailand's biggest national celebrations.
4) _____ In some areas of Bangkok, groups of Buddhist monks gather to receive gifts from local citizens.

UNDERSTANDING WHAT YOU READ

If you can, answer these questions from memory. If you cannot, look back at the article.

1) What does Thailand offer its citizens?

_____

2) In which holiday are the waterways lit up with millions of candles?

_____

3) What is the main ritual of the Songkran festival?

_____

4) What does this ritual signify and how is it used?

_____

REMEMBERING DETAILS

Write TRUE or FALSE under each statement. If the statement is false, write the statement correctly.

1) Muang Thai means Land of the Smiles.

_____

2) Thailand is the world's most populated nation.

_____

3) Visakha Puga is a festival celebrating the birth of Buddha.

_____

4) Kings often take a ceremonial bath to cleanse their spirits.

_____

INFERENCES

Based on the article, circle the letter of the best sentence completion.

1) Thailand's people are some of the proudest and friendliest in the world because...

a) Thailand has remained free.
b) Thailand is a modern and wealthy nation.
c) Thailand is a safe, stable and prosperous place to live.
d) all of the above.

2) Buddhist monks receive gifts from local citizens because...

a) they hope it will bring them good luck.
b) honor is paid to Buddha during Songkran.
c) it is a show of respect.
d) the monks need charity.

INTERPRETATION

1) Write a short paragraph describing how you think Thailand got each of its nicknames.

2) Thailand has never been conquered or colonized. Discuss with a partner possible reasons why Thailand has remained free.

3) Write a short composition explaining why citizens believe the release of birds and fish will bring them good luck.

WORD POWER

Circle the letter of the word that means the same as the word on the left.

1) fitting	a) happy	b) appropriate	c) desired
2) conquered	a) overpowered	b) surrendered	c) ruined
3) abundant	a) plentiful	b) lush	c) luxurious
4) stable	a) secure	b) common	c) good
5) symbolize	a) mirror	b) attain	c) represent
6) vendors	a) monks	b) citizens	c) peddlers

CROSSWORD PUZZLE

ACROSS:

1) The most fitting nickname for Thailand is Land of the _____.
3) Songkran is one time when Thailand lives up to its most fitting _____.
6) The people of Thailand are some of the _____, friendliest people in the world.
8) Marching bands play a _____ of musical instruments.
10) Thailand offers its citizens a safe, stable and _____ place in which to live.
13) Loy Krathong is a three-day event where _____ are lit up with candles.
14) The sprinkling of water is done to symbolize the _____ of the spirit.
15) Splashing water is a way of _____ a person your blessings.

DOWN:

2) Thailand is one of the most _____ and wealthy nations in Southeast Asia.
4) Water is sprinkled on Buddhist _____ during Songkran.
5) Some of Thailand's festivals hold important religious _____.
7) Thailand is a _____ nation.
9) Large groups of Buddhist _____ gather to receive gifts from local citizens.
11) Many of Songkran's rituals involve _____ each other with water.
12) Songkran is one of Thailand's biggest _____ celebrations.
14) Vendors can be found selling _____ birds and live fish.

18-5

ANSWER KEY

MAIN IDEAS vs SUPPORTING DETAILS

1) S
2) M
3) M
4) S

UNDERSTANDING WHAT YOU READ

1) Thailand offers its citizens a safe, stable and prosperous place in which to live, an excellent climate and a large Buddhist community.
2) During Loy Krathong the waterways are lit up with millions of candles.
3) The main ritual of the Songkran festival is the showering or sprinkling of water.
4) The sprinkling of water symbolizes the cleansing of the spirit and is used to show respect and to offer others blessings and wishes for happiness and good health.

REMEMBERING DETAILS

1) F   Muang Thai means Land of the Free.
2) F   China is the world's most populated nation.
3) T
4) F   Kings often take a ceremonial bath to honor Buddha.

INFERENCES

1) d
2) b

WORD POWER

1) b
2) a
3) a
4) a
5) c
6) c

CROSSWORD PUZZLE

ACROSS: 1) Smiles 2) nickname 6) proudest 8) variety 10) prosperous 13) waterways 14) cleansing 15) offering

DOWN: 2) modern 4) images 5) meaning 7) tropical 9) monks 11) showering 12) national 14) caged

Native American Day

1 In 1492, Italian explorer Christopher Columbus set sail from Spain in search of the New World. Although no one in the East knew it at the time, the world Columbus is credited with discovering was not an unsettled country. In fact, nearly one million Native people were already living north of the Mexican border when Columbus first travelled the southeast coast of America.

2 America's Native people had already developed their own civilization long before the arrival of white explorers from European countries. Nearly 600 distinct tribes of Native Americans lived, worked, farmed and hunted the vast regions of land that would eventually become the United States of America. Powerful nations like the Blackfoot, Sioux, Crow, Cheyenne, Omaha, Comanche and Apache could be found roaming freely, with nearly two-thirds of them on the Great Plains that stretched from Mexico to Canada.

3 For many of these nations, the buffalo provided a way of life. Herds of as many as 12 to 15 million buffalo could be found on the plains, and hunting them helped provide food, clothing and shelter to the Natives. For centuries, daily life on the plains centered around the buffalo hunt.

4 That began to change when white settlers began pushing west across the plains, claiming as their own land once held by Native nations. With the Colorado gold rush of 1859 and the building of the railways attracting more settlers, many tribes felt their

way of life being threatened. Railway workers began slaughtering thousands of buffalo, reducing the Native Americans' main source of food. During the 1840s and 1850s, the American army built a line of forts across the plains to protect traders, travellers and railroad workers from attack. From these forts, the army went to war with many tribes.

5   Fighting continued for many years, costing many white civilians and Native Americans their lives. In 1887, the American Congress passed the Dawes Act, forcing many Natives onto reservations and breaking up the tribe as the basic unit of Native American society. The arrival of the white man nearly 400 years earlier eventually cost many Native Americans the right to their homeland.

6   In 1914, one Native American decided it was time to recognize the contributions Natives had made to the country. Red Fox James, a member of the northern Blackfoot tribe, saddled up his horse and rode 4,000 miles across the nation to gain support for his idea. James wanted the government of the United States to set aside a special day in honor of all Native Americans. His request was endorsed by the governors of twenty-four states.

7   The first Native American Day was observed on the second Saturday of May in 1916. The names of great Native leaders like Sitting Bull, Crazy Horse and Geronimo were honored and peace pipe ceremonies were held.

8   Today, the states of Illinois, Arizona, California and Connecticut observe Native American's Day on the fourth Friday in September. In other parts of the country, the date of the celebration changes from year to year.

9   No matter what day it is held, Native American Day is a time to reflect on the rich history and often tragic story of the Native people in North America.

MAIN IDEAS vs. SUPPORTING DETAILS

The following sentences are either Main Ideas or Supporting Details. Put an "M" beside those that are Main Ideas, and an "S" beside those that are Supporting Details.

1) _____ In 1492, Columbus set sail from Spain to discover the New World.
2) _____ Native Americans had their own civilization before the arrival of white settlers.
3) _____ White settlers began claiming as their own land once held by Native American nations.
4) _____ In 1887, the American Congress passed the Dawes Act.

UNDERSTANDING WHAT YOU READ

If you can, answer these questions from memory. If you cannot, look back at the article.

1) How many distinct Native American tribes were there before the arrival of the white settlers in what would later become the United States ?

_____

2) Where were the majority of the Native American tribes located?

_____

3) Before the arrival of the white settlers, what was the Native way of life?

_____

4) How was Red Fox James significant to the Native Americans' cause?

_____

REMEMBERING DETAILS

Write TRUE or FALSE under each statement. If the statement is false, write the statement correctly.

1) When Christopher Columbus arrived in the New World, he found no people living there.

_____

2) During the Colorado gold rush, prospectors slaughtered thousands of buffalo.

_____

3) The first Native American Day was observed in 1914.

_____

4) In some parts of the United States the date of Native American Day changes from year to year.

_____

19-3

INFERENCES

Based on the article, circle the letter of the best sentence completion.

1) The buffalo were slaughtered because...

a) they were used as food during the Colorado gold rush.
b) soldiers enjoyed hunting.
c) there was a shortage of food for the railway workers.
d) they were interfering with the building of the railroad.

2) The army went to war with the Native Americans because...

a) the army wanted to control the buffalo herds.
b) the army wanted control of the land held by the Natives.
c) the army wanted to enslave the Native people.
d) the army wanted to emancipate the Natives.

INTERPRETATION

1) Discuss with a partner the effect the loss of the buffalo had on Native Americans.

2) Write a short composition outlining the reasons behind the passing of the Dawes Act by the American Congress.

3) Native Americans often had names taken from nature, such as Red Fox, Sitting Bull and Crazy Horse. If you were to choose a name from nature, what would it be? In small groups, tell each other your name and why you chose it.

WORD POWER

Circle the letter of the word that means the same as the word on the left.

1) explorer	a) statesman	b) adventurer	c) sailor
2) eventually	a) someday	b) never	c) soon
3) roaming	a) running	b) grazing	c) wandering
4) shelter	a) housing	b) refuge	c) water
5) basic	a) important	b) fundamental	c) radical
6) reflect	a) think	b) mirror	c) study

CROSSWORD PUZZLE

ACROSS:

3) James' request was _____ by the governors of twenty-four states.
4) Two-thirds of the Native American nations _____ on the Great Plains.
5) In 1942, Columbus set _____ from Spain in search of the New World.
6) Red Fox James was a member of the northern _____ tribe.
9) For many Native nations, the _____ provided a way of life.
10) Fighting continued for many years, _____ many people their lives.
12) For centuries, daily life on the _____ centered around the buffalo hunt.
14) Many Natives felt their way of life was being _____.

DOWN:

1) The Dawes Act forced many Natives onto _____.
2) The American army built a line of _____ across the plains.
5) Columbus travelled the _____ coast of America.
7) The first Native American Day was _____ in 1916.
8) The story of the Native people of North America is often _____.
10) White settlers began _____ as their own land once held by Native nations.
11) Red Fox James travelled across the nation to _____ support for his idea.
13) The Great Plains stretched from Mexico to _____.

19-5

ANSWER KEY

MAIN IDEAS vs SUPPORTING DETAILS

1) S
2) M
3) S
4) M

UNDERSTANDING WHAT YOU READ

1) There were nearly 600 distinct Native American tribes before the arrival of the white settlers in what would later become the United States.
2) The majority of the Native American tribes were located on the Great Plains that stretched between Mexico and Canada.
3) Before the arrival of white settlers the Native way of life centered around the buffalo, which provided them with food, clothing and shelter.
4) Red Fox James was significant to the Native Americans' cause because he was influential in the establishment of a special day to honor all Native Americans.

REMEMBERING DETAILS

1) F   Christopher Columbus discovered the New World was populated with Native Americans.
2) F   Railway workers slaughtered thousands of buffalo.
3) F   The first Native American Day was observed on the second Saturday of May in 1916.
4) T

INFERENCES

1) d
2) b

WORD POWER

1) b
2) a
3) c
4) a
5) b
6) a

CROSSWORD PUZZLE

ACROSS: 3) endorsed 4) lived 5) sail 6) Blackfoot 9) buffalo 10) costing 12) plains 14) threatened

DOWN: 1) reservations 2) forts 5) southeast 7) observed 8) tragic 10) claiming 11) gain 13) Canada

Yom Kippur

1 The Jewish faith regards ritual fasting as an important sign of devotion. Jewish people observe this ritual fast on a day called Yom Kippur. Also known as the Day of Atonement, Yom Kippur is a day when Jewish people show their faith to God and appeal for his forgiveness.

2 Yom Kippur is the holiest day in the Jewish calendar. It falls ten days after Rosh Hashanah, the Jewish New Year, and is the last of the Ten Days of Penitence. During these days, religious obligations are strictly observed; the Jewish people hope that by repentance of past sins, by prayer, and by charity, they may be thought well of by God in the Book of Life. It is believed that each person's actions are recorded in the Book of Life, and that their fate for the coming year is based on God's judgement of these actions.

3 The ninth of the Days of Penitence is a day of preparation for Yom Kippur, and the day is centered around the preparation and eating of festive meals. In this way, the people are strengthened for the coming fast.

4 In seeking God's forgiveness, it is important to seek the forgiveness of others. For this reason on the ninth of the Days of Penitence, people ask their friends and neighbors for pardon from any past transgressions.

5 In Israel, the sound of a soft siren announces the beginning of Yom Kippur; this takes place at sundown on

the ninth Day of Penitence. At this signal, people begin making their way to the synagogue to worship; on the way they embrace their friends and neighbors. It is traditional to say to a friend "may you be well inscribed"; this saying is a wish that they be looked upon kindly by God when He remembers them in the Book of Life.

6   For the twenty-four hours of Yom Kippur, it is forbidden to take any food or drink, or to engage in marital relations. Traditionally, bathing is also prohibited, as is the wearing of leather shoes. These are seen as "afflictions" of the soul, as not appropriate to a condition of holiness, and therefore as preventing a closeness to God. It is also traditional for white clothes to be worn--as in many other cultures, white symbolizes purity.

7   The more observant of Jewish people will spend the entire twenty-four hours in the synagogue, praying and participating in services which begin right at sundown. For the time spent in the synagogue, the worshipper is oblivious to the outside world, and so is closer to God.

8   The importance of this closeness can be seen in one of the customs observed toward the end of Yom Kippur. A special service known as "Ne'ilah" signals the closing of the gates of heaven, which have been open all day to receive prayers. This marks the most solemn part of the day, and at this time it is not uncommon for worshippers to stand throughout this hour-long service, in a final attempt to be close to God.

9   At sunset, the blowing of a ceremonial horn, the shofar, signals the end of Yom Kippur, and the breaking of the fast. This is a time of great happiness for having been purified of past sins and for having received the pardon of God.

MAIN IDEAS vs. SUPPORTING DETAILS

The following sentences are either Main Ideas or Supporting Details. Put an "M" beside those that are Main Ideas, and an "S" beside those that are Supporting Details.

1) _____ Yom Kippur is the last day of the Ten Days of Penitence.
2) _____ During Yom Kippur, religious obligations are strictly observed.
3) _____ Towards the end of Yom Kippur, there is a special hour-long service called Ne'ilah.
4) _____ The Jewish people hope to get closer to God through praying and participating in services during Yom Kippur.

UNDERSTANDING WHAT YOU READ

If you can, answer these questions from memory. If you cannot, look back at the article.

1) As what do Jewish people regard fasting?

_____

2) What is Yom Kippur?

_____

3) Who do people ask for forgiveness on the ninth of the Days of Penitence?

_____

4) What signals the beginning of Yom Kippur in Israel?

_____

REMEMBERING DETAILS

Write TRUE or FALSE under each statement. If the statement is false, write the statement correctly.

1) Yom Kippur is the Jewish New Year.

_____

2) Yom Kippur lasts two days.

_____

3) During Yom Kippur bathing is not permitted.

_____

4) The most festive part of Yom Kippur is "Ne'ilah."

_____

INFERENCES

Based on the article, circle the letter of the best sentence completion.

1) Jewish people feel ritual fasting is an important sign of devotion because...

a) it is an appeal to God for forgiveness.
b) to go hungry is to know one's human frailty.
c) it makes them realize their dependence on God.
d) it is part of Yom Kippur.

2) Bathing and the wearing of leather shoes are prohibited during Yom Kippur because...

a) they are seen as afflictions of the soul.
b) they prevent a closeness to God.
c) they are not appropriate to a condition of holiness.
d) all of the above.

INTERPRETATION

1) With a partner, brainstorm reasons why you think white is a symbol of purity in many cultures.

2) Have you ever fasted? Why did you? For how long? What were your experiences? Write a short composition answering these questions.

3) Rituals are important to many religions and cultures. Why? Discuss.

WORD POWER

Circle the letter of the word that means the same as the word on the left.

1) appeal	a) summon	b) plead	c) address
2) obligations	a) responsibilities	b) compulsions	c) contracts
3) oblivious	a) preoccupied	b) careless	c) unaware
4) customs	a) rules	b) traditions	c) fashions
5) solemn	a) active	b) sociable	c) serious
6) purified	a) wash	b) refined	c) cleansed

CROSSWORD PUZZLE

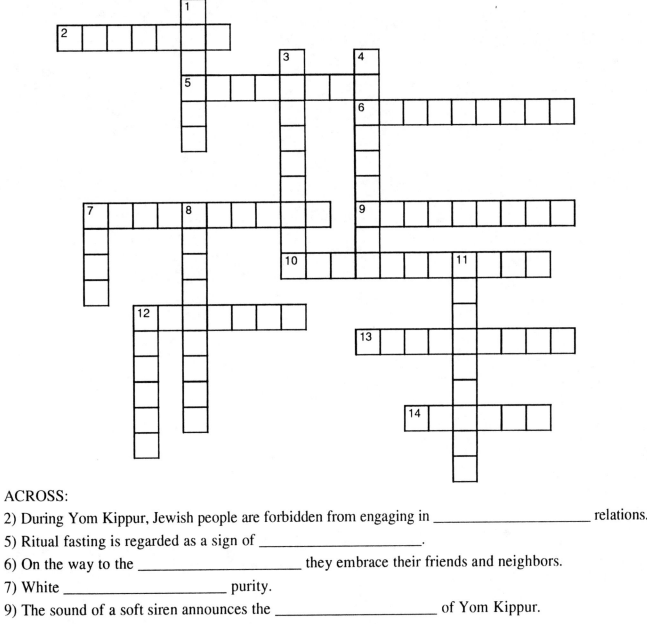

ACROSS:
2) During Yom Kippur, Jewish people are forbidden from engaging in _____ relations.
5) Ritual fasting is regarded as a sign of _____.
6) On the way to the _____ they embrace their friends and neighbors.
7) White _____ purity.
9) The sound of a soft siren announces the _____ of Yom Kippur.
10) It is _____ to wear white clothes.
12) At the end of Yom Kippur there is a special _____ known as Ne'ilah.
13) The end of Yom Kippur is a time of great _____.
14) At sunset the _____ is blown.

DOWN:
1) People ask their friends for _____ from any past transgressions.
3) Yom Kippur is also known as the Day of _____.
4) "May you be well _____."
7) During Yom Kippur, _____ are confessed.
8) The more _____ Jewish people spend the entire Yom Kippur in prayer.
11) At the synagogue the worshipper is _____ to the outside world.
12) Ne'ilah is the most _____ part of the last day.

20-5

ANSWER KEY

MAIN IDEAS vs SUPPORTING DETAILS

1) S
2) S
3) M
4) M

UNDERSTANDING WHAT YOU READ

1) Jewish people regard fasting as an important sign of devotion.
2) Yom Kippur is the holiest day in the Jewish calendar. It is also known as the Day of Atonement. Yom Kippur is a day when Jewish people show their faith to God and appeal for his forgiveness.
3) On the ninth of the Days of Penitence, Jewish people ask for forgiveness from God, their friends and their neighbors.
4) In Israel the sound of a a soft siren signals the beginning of Yom Kippur.

REMEMBERING DETAILS

1) F   Yom Kippur is ten days after the Jewish New Year. The Jewish New Year is Rosh Hashanah.
2) F   Yom Kippur lasts twenty-four hours.
3) T
4) F   "Ne'ilah" is the most solemn part of Yom Kippur.

INFERENCES

1) c
2) d

WORD POWER

1) b
2) a
3) c
4) b
5) c
6) c

CROSSWORD PUZZLE

ACROSS: 2) marital 5) devotion 6) synagogue 7) symbolizes 9) beginning 10) traditional 12) service 13) happiness 14) shofar

DOWN: 1) pardon 3) Atonement 4) inscribed 7) sins 8) observant 11) oblivious 12) solemn

Rizal Day

1. The history of any country is the story of many great people. In the Philippines, one person who helped shape Philippine history is celebrated annually on Rizal Day.

2. Rizal Day is named for Dr. Jose Rizal, a hero and figure of inspiration for the people of the Philippines. Held on the anniversary of Rizal's death, Rizal Day is a solemn day of tribute to his life.

3. Jose Rizal lived at a time when the Philippines were ruled by the Spanish, and he was outspoken in his opposition to the government and its belief that the people of the Philippines were inferior to the Spanish. He wrote two novels dramatizing the abuses of the Spanish rulers; both novels were banned in his own country. Rizal eventually became known as the leader of a reform movement to establish the Philippines as an independent nation.

4. Educated in Europe, Rizal is also an example to all Filipinos for his achievements as a surgeon, a botanist, a writer, a sculptor and an educator. Rizal could also speak six languages.

5. Although Rizal promoted a peaceful reform which would allow equal status for the Spanish and the Filipinos, at the beginning of the 1896 revolution for Philippine independence he was identified as an accomplice of those who would violently overthrow the government. He was arrested and, after a brief trial, was executed before a firing squad.

6   An independent Philippines was established two years later. One of the new government's first acts was to proclaim a special day to mark Rizal's execution; Rizal Day was made a national holiday to take place every December thirtieth.

7   Memorials commemorating Jose Rizal have since been built in many towns, a province has been named for him, and his novels, once banned, are legally required reading for Filipino college students.

8   Ceremonies marking Rizal Day are held throughout the country. Flags fly at half-mast in his memory. At the Rizal Monument in Manila, the capital of the Philippines, Rizal Day is observed with the presentation of speeches celebrating Rizal's life and his contributions to Philippine history. The tone of the ceremony is generally somber, yet Rizal Day is a day of great pride for the people of the Philippines.

9   Each year Rizal Day offers the Philippine people an opportunity to strongly assert their cherished independence. This sense of the importance of their independence grew further throughout the more modern years of struggle against the influence of the United States, which saw the Philippines as a place of strategic importance for military concerns. For this reason, the speeches presented at the official Rizal Day ceremony are delivered in the native language of the Philippines, Tagalog, rather than the English that the Americans promoted through the education system.

10   Rizal Day ceremonies traditionally end with readings of Rizal's poem, "Ultima Adios," which means last farewell. The poem was composed on the night before Rizal's execution, and it holds a special place in the culture of the Philippines: many students learn to recite "Ultima Adios" from memory.

MAIN IDEAS vs. SUPPORTING DETAILS

The following sentences are either Main Ideas or Supporting Details. Put an "M" beside those that are Main Ideas, and an "S" beside those that are Supporting Details.

1) _____ Rizal wrote two novels dramatizing the abuses of the Spaniards.
2) _____ Ceremonies marking Rizal Day are held throughout the country.
3) _____ The tone of Rizal Day ceremonies are generally somber.
4) _____ Rizal Day is a day of great pride for the people of the Philippines.

UNDERSTANDING WHAT YOU READ

If you can, answer these questions from memory. If you cannot, look back at the article.

1) How did Jose Rizal help shape Philippine history?

_____

2) How long after Rizal's execution did the Philippines gain independence?

_____

3) Who reads Rizal's novels?

_____

4) How did the United States view the Philippines? What effect did this have on the celebration of Rizal Day?

_____

REMEMBERING DETAILS

Write TRUE or FALSE under each statement. If the statement is false, write the statement correctly.

1) Rizal's idea for reform promoted the superiority of the Philippine people.

_____

2) In 1896, Rizal was identified as an accomplice to those who wanted to overthrow the Spanish government.

_____

3) Ceremonies marking Rizal Day are only held in the Philippine capital of Manila.

_____

4) "Ultima Adios" was written as a memorial to Jose Rizal.

_____

21-3

INFERENCES

Based on the article, circle the letter of the best sentence completion.

1) The Philippines sought independence from the Spanish because...

a) the Filipinos wanted their own form of government.
b) the Spanish abused the Filipinos and believed they were inferior.
c) the Spanish executed Jose Rizal.
d) the Spanish had banned Rizal's novels.

2) Rizal was executed because...

a) the Spanish identified him as an accomplice of those who wanted to overthrow the government
b) the Spanish felt he had betrayed them.
c) the Spanish disliked the poem he had composed.
d) the Spanish believed he started the 1896 revolution.

INTERPRETATION

1) Jose Rizal was a hero and figure of inspiration for the people of the Philippines. Do you have your own hero or figure of inspiration? Write a short composition describing this person.

2) Rizal spoke six languages. Do you think that this is an accomplishment? Do you think it would be hard to learn six languages? Discuss your ideas with a partner.

3) Do you think it is acceptable for a government to ban books and novels? Under what conditions, or for what types of books would this be acceptable?

WORD POWER

Circle the letter of the word that means the same as the word on the left.

1) shape	a) start	b) produce	c) mold
2) figure	a) symbol	b) calculate	c) pattern
3) abuses	a) adventures	b) exploitations	c) impositions
4) banned	a) tolerated	b) prohibited	c) authorized
5) accomplice	a) collaborator	b) friend	c) spy
6) tone	a) temper	b) color	c) mood

CROSSWORD PUZZLE

ACROSS:
3) Rizal Day celebrates Dr. Jose Rizal's life and his _____ to Philippine history.
6) Dr. Jose Rizal is a _____ and a figure of inspiration to Filipinos.
9) Rizal was _____ in his opposition to the Spanish government.
12) Rizal was identified with those who would violently _____ the government.
15) Rizal's novels were once _____ in the Philippines.
16) "Ultima Adios" was _____ on the night before Rizal's execution.

DOWN:
1) Memorials _____ Jose Rizal have been built in many towns.
2) Rizal Day offers Filipinos an opportunity to strongly _____ their independence.
4) The _____ of Rizal Day is generally somber.
5) Rizal Day is a solemn day of _____ to Jose Rizal's life.
7) Rizal was also a _____, surgeon and an educator.
8) Rizal became known as the leader of the _____ movement.
10) The United States saw the Philippines as a place of _____ importance.
11) One of the first acts of the new government was to _____ Rizal Day.
13) After a brief trial, Rizal was _____ before a firing squad.
14) Rizal Day is a day of great _____ for the people of the Philippines.

21-5

ANSWER KEY

MAIN IDEAS vs SUPPORTING DETAILS

1) S
2) M
3) S
4) M

UNDERSTANDING WHAT YOU READ

1) Jose Rizal helped shape Philippine history in many ways. First, he opposed the Spanish government and its abuses. Next, he wrote novels documenting those abuses. Finally, he became the leader of a reform movement that promoted peaceful reforms. In the end he was executed for his beliefs.
2) The establishment of an independent Philippines happened two years after Rizal's execution.
3) Rizal's novels were once banned, but are now required reading for Filipino college students.
4) The United States saw the Philippines as a place of strategic importance for military concerns and, as a result, speeches on Rizal Day are delivered in Tagalog.

REMEMBERING DETAILS

1) F   Rizal's idea for reform promoted equal status for the Spanish and the Filipinos.
2) T
3) F   Ceremonies marking Rizal Day are held throughout the country, including Manila.
4) F   "Ultima Adios" was written by Jose Rizal on the night before his execution.

INFERENCES

1) b
2) a

WORD POWER

1) c
2) a
3) b
4) b
5) a
6) c

CROSSWORD PUZZLE

ACROSS: 3) contributions 6) hero 9) outspoken 12) overthrow 15) banned 16) composed

DOWN: 1) commemorating 2) assert 4) tone 5) tribute 7) botanist 8) reform 10) strategic 11) proclaim 13) executed 14) pride

International Day of Peace

1   It would be difficult to find somebody who would not like to see a world without war. While this may be true, peace still seems a distant goal in a world which continues to be divided by conflict.

2   The United Nations, in "recognizing that peace continues to be a goal instead of an achievement," declared an annual observation of this desire for world peace. This day is known as the International Day of Peace.

3   The United Nations is a collective organization of 178 countries. Founded in 1945, shortly after the end of World War II, the U.N. was originally made up of countries that had stood against Germany, Italy and Japan in the Second World War. These fifty countries came together to find a way to ensure that such a war never occurred again. A document called the Charter of the United Nations was drawn up by these countries which set out a concrete plan for the maintenance of peace.

4   The Charter of the United Nations contains the purposes and principles by which the U.N. is organized and operated. The first purpose of the Charter is the preservation of world peace and security. This is to be achieved through the cooperation and tolerance of the U.N.'s member countries, and through the deployment of peace-keeping forces to prevent the eruption of war where conflict exists. In addition, studies about the causes of war and the possibilities of peace are

carried out on a continuous basis.

5   On November 30, 1981, the General Assembly--the main organizing body of the United Nations--proclaimed an International Day of Peace. The Day was to be observed every year on the third Tuesday in September, coinciding with the opening day of the General Assembly's regular session.

6   The International Day of Peace is designated to draw world attention to the continuing struggle for world peace. The Day of Peace is an acknowledgement of both the work that has been done, and the work that remains to be done in the cause of peace. Each member country in the U.N. is invited to participate in its own way, but especially through education. Individuals, municipalities and non-government bodies are also urged to take part in observing Peace Day. The U.N. sets a different theme for each year's observance, and special events are to be organized around this theme.

7   At the United Nations' headquarters in New York City, the U.N. Secretary General delivers a special message commemorating that year's Day of Peace; he then rings a Peace Bell, and he invokes a time of reflection to be shared by the people of the world.

8   On the twenty-fourth of October, 1985--the fortieth anniversary of the United Nations--an International Year of Peace was declared for 1986. The year-long observance was to emphasize more forcefully the ongoing cause of world peace. Special events and observances were held by various countries around the world.

9   Our wish should continue to be that the people of the world should live in peace and security; we should wish that there was no need for an International Day of Peace.

MAIN IDEAS vs. SUPPORTING DETAILS

The following sentences are either Main Ideas or Supporting Details. Put an "M" beside those that are Main Ideas, and an "S" beside those that are Supporting Details.

1) _____ It is difficult to find a person who would not like to see peace.
2) _____ The International Day of Peace was declared to observe the world's desire for peace.
3) _____ The United Nations was formed in 1945, shortly after the end of World War II.
4) _____ The U.N. sets a theme for each year's observance.

UNDERSTANDING WHAT YOU READ

If you can, answer these questions from memory. If you cannot, look back at the article.

1) Who were the original members of the United Nations?

_____

2) What is the first purpose of the Charter of the United Nations?

_____

3) When was the International Day of Peace first proclaimed?

_____

4) What happened on the fortieth anniversary of the United Nations?

_____

REMEMBERING DETAILS

Write TRUE or FALSE under each statement. If the statement is false, write the statement correctly.

1) The United Nations recognizes that, for the most part, the world has achieved peace.

_____

2) The United Nations is made up of fifty countries.

_____

3) The Charter of the U.N. states that studies about the possibilities for world peace are to be carried out on a continuous basis.

_____

4) The International Day of Peace is observed annually on November 30th.

_____

INFERENCES

Based on the article, circle the letter of the best sentence completion.

1) The U.N. needs the cooperation and tolerance of its members because...

a) it needs their armies for peace-keeping missions.
b) conflict between neighboring countries is inevitable.
c) it wants the International Day of Peace to be celebrated worldwide.
d) it wants to maintain world peace.

2) The International Day of Peace is designated to draw world attention to the continuing struggle for world peace because...

a) that is the mandate of the Charter of the United Nations.
b) the United Nations does not want another world war.
c) peace remains a distant goal in a world which continues to be divided by conflict.
d) education is needed as to the causes of war and the possibilities for peace.

INTERPRETATION

1) What type of education should the U.N. provide about the causes of war and the possibilities of peace? Write a letter to the U.N. Secretary General outlining your suggestions for ways to achieve world peace.

2) Is there still a need for an International Day of Peace? Prepare a short presentation for your class on your views.

3) Why do you think peace is still a distant goal? Discuss your ideas with a partner.

WORD POWER

Circle the letter of the word that means the same as the word on the left.

1) founded	a) established	b) deployed	c) supported
2) concrete	a) firm	b) indefinite	c) variable
3) maintenance	a) subsistence	b) preservation	c) declaration
4) deployment	a) strength	b) tolerance	c) use
5) draw	a) pull	b) attract	c) collect
6) commemorating	a) observing	b) keeping	c) beginning

CROSSWORD PUZZLE

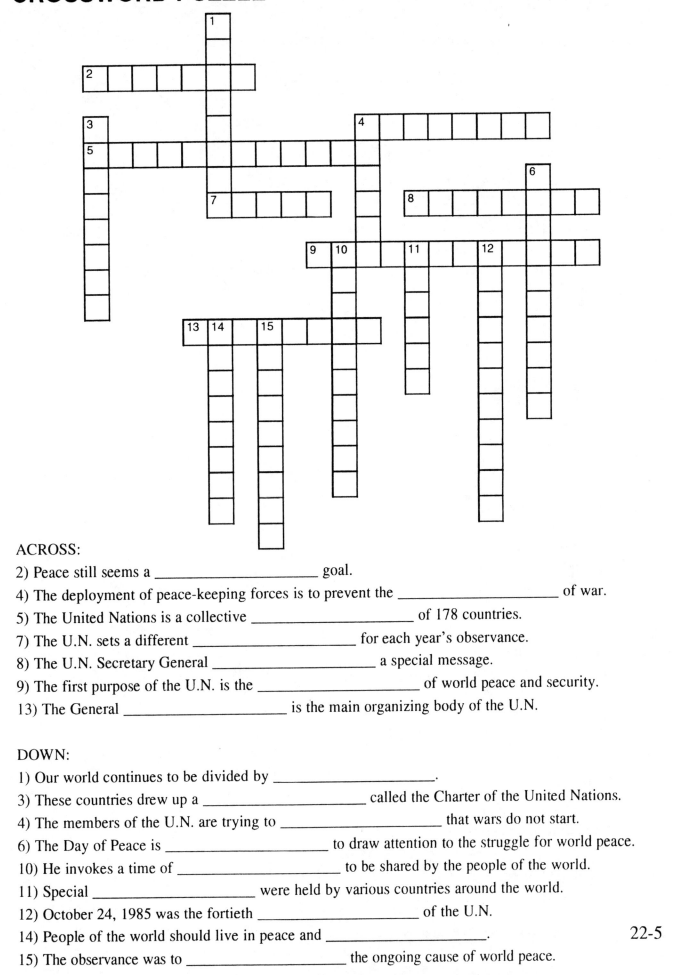

ACROSS:

2) Peace still seems a _____ goal.
4) The deployment of peace-keeping forces is to prevent the _____ of war.
5) The United Nations is a collective _____ of 178 countries.
7) The U.N. sets a different _____ for each year's observance.
8) The U.N. Secretary General _____ a special message.
9) The first purpose of the U.N. is the _____ of world peace and security.
13) The General _____ is the main organizing body of the U.N.

DOWN:

1) Our world continues to be divided by _____.
3) These countries drew up a _____ called the Charter of the United Nations.
4) The members of the U.N. are trying to _____ that wars do not start.
6) The Day of Peace is _____ to draw attention to the struggle for world peace.
10) He invokes a time of _____ to be shared by the people of the world.
11) Special _____ were held by various countries around the world.
12) October 24, 1985 was the fortieth _____ of the U.N.
14) People of the world should live in peace and _____.
15) The observance was to _____ the ongoing cause of world peace.

22-5

ANSWER KEY

MAIN IDEAS vs SUPPORTING DETAILS

1) S
2) M
3) S
4) S

UNDERSTANDING WHAT YOU READ

1) The United Nations was originally made up of the fifty countries that had stood against Germany, Japan and Italy during World War II.
2) The first purpose of the Charter of the United Nations is the preservation of world peace and security.
3) The International Day of Peace was first proclaimed on November 30, 1981.
4) On October 24, 1985, the fortieth anniversary of the United Nations, an International Year of Peace was declared for 1986.

REMEMBERING DETAILS

1) F   The United Nations recognizes that peace continues to be a goal instead of an achievement.
2) F   The United Nations is a collective organization of 178 countries.
3) T
4) F   The International Day of Peace is observed annually on the third Tuesday in September.

INFERENCES

1) d
2) c

WORD POWER

1) a
2) a
3) b
4) c
5) b
6) a

CROSSWORD PUZZLE

ACROSS: 2) distant 4) eruption 5) organization 7) theme 8) delivers 9) preservation 13) Assembly

DOWN: 1) conflict 3) document 4) ensure 6) designated 10) reflection 11) events 12) anniversary 14) security 15) emphasize

Carnival

1   Carnival is a huge celebration taking place in the days leading up to the Christian period of Lent. While Carnival is observed in various parts of Europe and North and South America, the wild and expressive Brazilian festival is the most famous.

2   Lent is a forty day period leading up to Easter; during Lent penance is to be made for past sins in preparation for the observance of Christ's death and resurrection. While in the past Lent took the form of strict fasting, today the prohibitions are more relaxed. However, Lent still remains a time of self-denial and prayer.

3   The name Carnival refers to the prohibition of meat during Lent: "carnival" is rooted in the Latin "carnem lavare," meaning "to take away meat."

4   Carnival has been celebrated for centuries in Europe. Traditionally, the celebration included parades, masked dances or balls and great feasts. Colorful costumes always play a big part in Carnival celebrations, and perhaps add to the loosening of inhibitions which contrast so sharply with the solemn period to come.

5   Carnival arrived in North and South America with the European settlers, and in Brazil the celebration has grown to be one of the biggest and most famous festivals in the world. In both the cities and the countryside, Carnival is Brazil's major holiday, and preparation for the festivities

sometimes begin almost a year in advance.

6   Carnival in Brazil began with the Portuguese settlers in the seventeenth century, and the tradition was adopted by the black slaves that had been brought there. Since that time, Carnival has grown to become an expression of Brazilian culture, and has represented a relaxation of everyday rules. In a country with sharp divisions between economic classes, rich and poor alike participate in Carnival celebrations.

7   The most lavish celebration takes place in Rio de Janeiro, Brazil's largest city. Since the 1930s, the party has taken the form of a massive display of colorful costumes and loud music. The music played in homes, nightclubs and on street corners is known as samba.

8   Samba is the musical expression of Carnival. The major participants in Rio's parades and pageants are neighborhood groups known as samba schools, and Carnival reaches its high point with a competition among these groups. Each samba school invents its own theme for each year's competition, with specially composed music and dances, and costumes designed to fit the theme. The groups travel down Rio's main street on decorated floats, enacting their theme, and are judged by an awards committee.

9   The parade leads to the Sambadrome, a stadium designed specifically for this event. In the stadium, the party continues throughout the night, with all the samba schools collected there with eighty-five thousand spectators; millions more watch on television.

10 In the United States, Carnival is celebrated in New Orleans, and is called Mardi Gras, which means fat Tuesday. Mardi Gras follows the French traditions of costumed parades and masked balls.

11 In Canada, Carnival is celebrated in Quebec City, with a distinctly winter flavor. Attractions include a castle built of ice, and a competition of ice sculptures.

MAIN IDEAS vs. SUPPORTING DETAILS

The following sentences are either Main Ideas or Supporting Details. Put an "M" beside those that are Main Ideas, and an "S" beside those that are Supporting Details.

1) _____ Carnival is observed in various parts of Europe and North and South America.
2) _____ While in the past Lent took the form of strict fasting, today the prohibitions are more relaxed.
3) _____ In both the cities and the countryside, Carnival is Brazil's major holiday.
4) _____ Each samba school invents its own theme for each year's competition.

UNDERSTANDING WHAT YOU READ

If you can, answer these questions from memory. If you cannot, look back at the article.

1) Where is Carnival celebrated ?

_____

2) What does the name Carnival mean ?

_____

3) How is Carnival celebrated in Brazil?

_____

4) What is samba and what is its role in Carnival?

_____

REMEMBERING DETAILS

Write TRUE or FALSE under each statement. If the statement is false, write the statement correctly.

1) Lent is a time for celebration.

_____

2) Carnival has been celebrated in Brazil with colorful costumes and loud music since the seventeenth century.

_____

3) Millions of people watch the party at the Sambadrome on television.

_____

4) In Canada, Carnival celebrations include a competition of snow castles.

_____

INFERENCES

Based on the article, circle the letter of the best sentence completion.

1) The most famous Carnival celebration is the Brazilian festival because...

a) it is an expression of Brazilian culture.
b) it is wild and expressive.
c) of the samba music.
d) it involves a massive display of colorful costumes.

2) Preparations for Carnival festivities begin almost a year in advance because...

a) Brazilians can only find the time to plan for Carnival while on their vacations.
b) planning in advance is also a feature of the Brazilian culture.
c) of the amount of time needed to develop annual themes, special costumes and specially composed music.
d) the Sambadrome is a busy stadium and it must be reserved well before Carnival.

INTERPRETATION

1) Does the wearing of colorful costumes and dancing to loud music, as in Brazilian Carnival, loosen inhibitions? Write a short composition supporting your answer.

2) If you were an owner of a samba school, what theme would you plan for next year's Carnival? Describe your theme in detail and then share it with your class.

3) With a partner, brainstorm possible reasons why Mardi Gras means fat Tuesday.

WORD POWER

Circle the letter of the word that means the same as the word on the left.

1) expressive	a) energetic	b) crazy	c) strange
2) rooted	a) based	b) removed	c) fixed
3) contrast	a) reflect	b) adds to	c) differ
4) in advance	a) further ahead	b) ahead of	c) further back
5) division	a) distribution	b) segment	c) separation
6) lavish	a) extravagant	b) wasteful	c) cheap

CROSSWORD PUZZLE

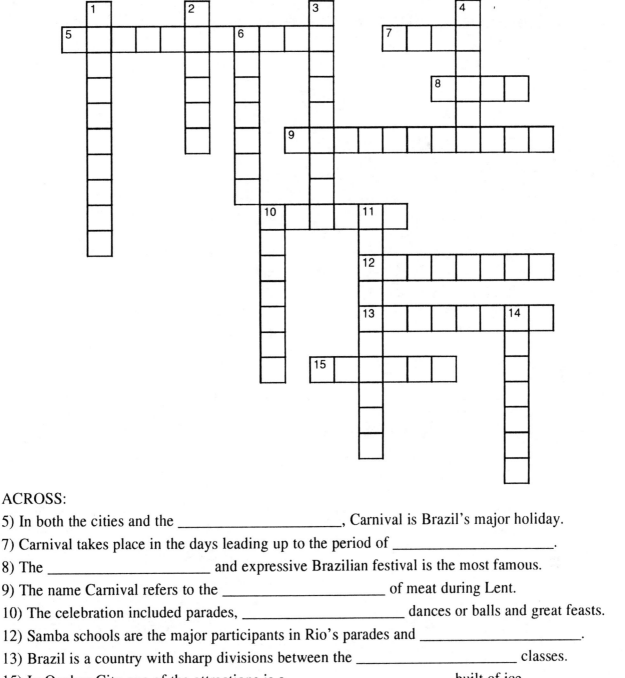

ACROSS:
5) In both the cities and the _____, Carnival is Brazil's major holiday.
7) Carnival takes place in the days leading up to the period of _____.
8) The _____ and expressive Brazilian festival is the most famous.
9) The name Carnival refers to the _____ of meat during Lent.
10) The celebration included parades, _____ dances or balls and great feasts.
12) Samba schools are the major participants in Rio's parades and _____.
13) Brazil is a country with sharp divisions between the _____ classes.
15) In Quebec City one of the attractions is a _____ built of ice.

DOWN:
1) Carnival began with the _____ settlers in the seventeenth century.
2) Mardi Gras follows the _____ traditions of costumed parades and masked balls.
3) Carnival has been celebrated for _____ in Europe.
4) In the past Lent took the form of _____ fasting.
6) The Sambadrome is a _____ specially designed for the samba competition.
10) Carnival has taken the form of a _____ display of costumes and music.
11) Carnival has grown to be an _____ of Brazilian culture.
14) Each samba school _____ its own theme for each year's competition.

23-5

ANSWER KEY

MAIN IDEAS vs. SUPPORTING DETAILS

1) S
2) S
3) M
4) S

UNDERSTANDING WHAT YOU READ

1) Carnival is celebrated in various parts of Europe and North and South America; the article references are to France, Portugal, Brazil, the United States and Canada.
2) The name Carnival refers to the prohibition of meat during Lent: carnival is rooted in the Latin "carnem lavare," meaning "to take away meat."
3) In Brazil, Carnival involves a massive display of colorful costumes and loud music. The music played at Carnival is known as samba. There are parades, pageants and samba competitions.
4) Samba is the musical expression of Carnival. There are samba schools that compete each year in Carnival's parades and pageants, with specially designed music and costumes, that are judged by an awards committee.

REMEMBERING DETAILS

1) F   Even though the prohibitions surrounding Lent are more relaxed than in the past, Lent remains a time of self-denial and prayer.
2) F   Carnival began in Brazil in the seventeenth century with the Portuguese settlers, but it was not until the 1930s that the celebration took its present form of massive displays of colorful costumes and loud music.
3) T
4) F   In Canada, Carnival celebrations include a castle built of ice and a competition of ice sculptures.

INFERENCES

1) b
2) c

WORD POWER

1) a
2) a
3) c
4) b
5) c
6) a

CROSSWORD PUZZLE

ACROSS: 5) countryside 7) Lent 8) wild 9) prohibition 10) masked 12) pageants 13) economic 15) castle

DOWN: 1) Portuguese 2) French 3) centuries 4) strict 6) stadium 10) massive 11) expression 14) invents

Khordad Sal

1   Zoroastrianism is one of the most ancient religions, dating back over two thousand years. The Zoroastrians have their origins in Iran, which at one time was called Persia. After being driven from Persia by advancing Muslim Arabs, the Zoroastrians mostly settled in India and became known as Parsis.

2   The founder of the religion of the Zoroastrians and Parsis was Zoroaster, or Zarathustra, as this prophet is also known. Although there is some debate as to the exact date, it is speculated that Zoroaster was born around 630 BC. The celebration of Zoroaster's birth takes place on Khordad Sal.

3   Khordad Sal designates the first day of the new year. "Khordad" is the name of the sixth day of the month Frawardin, and is the name of the God who looks after the year, month, day and time. The word "Sal" means "year," and "Khordad Sal" means "Khordad, lord of the year." Honor is to be paid to Khordad, in the hope that he will bring happiness in the coming year. The New Year is also known as No Ruz or Havzoru.

4   Khordad Sal is then both the day of the new year, and the birthday of Zoroaster. For the Zoroastrians, many significant events in the religion's history are believed to have occurred on New Year's Day. Although Khordad Sal is one of the most anticipated days of the Parsis calendar, the different sects place varying degrees of emphasis on the day as the birthday of Zoroaster.

5   On the day of Khordad Sal, worshippers are to pay respect to God with prayer. The day begins at dawn with ritual bathing, to purify the body and to prepare for the new clothes that will be worn on that day. Traditionally, seven articles of new clothing are to be worn on this day. A special prayer to the sun is recited nine times, and another prayer is recited three times to Mihr, the god of the sun.

6   Yet, despite the pious nature of these observances, families and communities look forward to the New Year festivities for the great feast to come. From early in the morning, women gather in the house of the village's priest. Each women brings a small copper bowl with a melon, a cucumber and an egg inside, as well as a selection of other fruits and vegetables. They also bring a list of those in their household over the age of nine: for each of these people the priest will say a prayer.

7   With all the food they have brought, the women prepare a great feast, which will be distributed among the community. All the food is blessed by the priest. Bread is baked. The eggs are boiled and peeled. The melon and cucumber are cut in half, with one half of each to be taken to the local temple to be distributed at a special service attended by the men of the village. The fresh bread is divided among the women and taken home to be eaten by their families. Each woman also drinks some consecrated water, and takes a bowl full home for her husband to drink. The rest of the food is divided among those at the priest's house.

8   Khordad Sal is a special celebration for the more than 175,000 Parsis worldwide, as it is one of both solemn prayer and joyous anticipation of the year to come.

MAIN IDEAS vs. SUPPORTING DETAILS

The following sentences are either Main Ideas or Supporting Details. Put an "M" beside those that are Main Ideas, and an "S" beside those that are Supporting Details.

1) _____ The New Year is also known as No Ruz or Havzoru.
2) _____ Worshippers pay respect to God with prayer on Khordad Sal.
3) _____ On Khordad Sal the day begins with ritual bathing.
4) _____ A great feast is part of the festivities of Khordad Sal.

UNDERSTANDING WHAT YOU READ

If you can, answer these questions from memory. If you cannot, look back at the article.

1) From where in the world do Zoroastrians originate?

_____

2) What is the most anticipated day of the Parsis calendar?

_____

3) Where is the feast for Khordad Sal prepared?

_____

4) Why do the women bring the priest a list of all those in their household over the age of nine?

_____

REMEMBERING DETAILS

Write TRUE or FALSE under each statement. If the statement is false, write the statement correctly.

1) The Zoroastrians were driven from Iran by the Parsis.

_____

2) Honor is paid to Khordad in the hope that he will bring wealth and prosperity in the coming year.

_____

3) Each women brings a pineapple, a carrot and a chicken to the village priest's house.

_____

4) Each woman drinks some consecrated water, and takes some home for her husband to drink.

_____

INFERENCES

Based on the article, circle the letter of the best sentence completion.

1) The different sects might celebrate the day differently because...

a) different regions use different calendars.
b) not all sects recognize Zoroaster as their prophet.
c) the different sects place varying degrees of emphasis on Khordad Sal as the birthday of Zoroaster.
d) there is some debate as to the exact date Zoroaster was born.

2) The day of Khordad Sal begins with ritual bathing because...

a) the worshippers take a bath before praying to Mihr.
b) they must get ready for the great feast that follows.
c) it is Zoroaster's birthday.
d) the worshippers must purify their bodies and prepare for the new clothes that will be worn on that day.

INTERPRETATION

1) Do you feel the way the food is distributed is significant? Discuss your reasons with a partner.

2) Discuss with a partner whether or not you believe certain numbers (e.g. the use of three, seven and nine for the Zoroastrians) carry importance?

3) Many celebrations worldwide include feasts. Brainstorm a list of possible reasons why this is a common practice in many cultures.

WORD POWER

Circle the letter of the word that means the same as the word on the left.

1) most ancient	a) youngest	b) oldest	c) most obsolete
2) exile	a) expulsion	b) separation	c) loss
3) dispersion	a) evaporation	b) scattering	c) dismissal
4) ritual	a) common	b) religious	c) ceremonial
5) pious	a) religious	b) customary	c) everyday
6) joyous	a) fun-loving	b) happy	c) anticipated

CROSSWORD PUZZLE

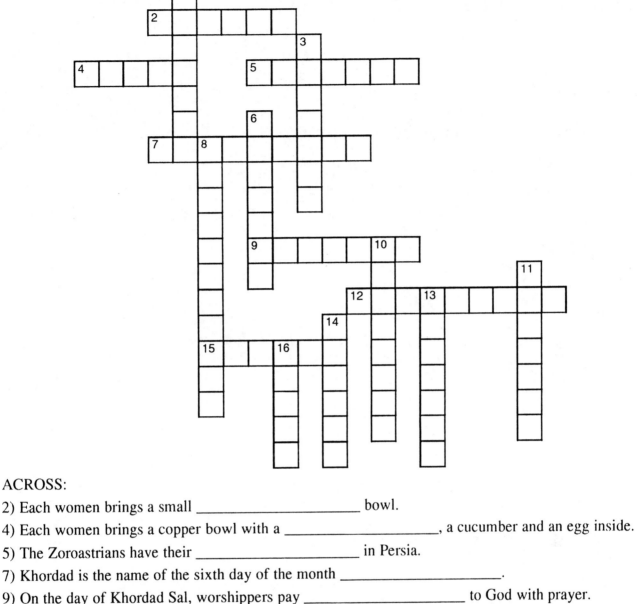

ACROSS:
2) Each women brings a small _____ bowl.
4) Each women brings a copper bowl with a _____, a cucumber and an egg inside.
5) The Zoroastrians have their _____ in Persia.
7) Khordad is the name of the sixth day of the month _____.
9) On the day of Khordad Sal, worshippers pay _____ to God with prayer.
12) Each woman brings a list of those in her _____ over the age of nine.
15) One half of the melon and cucumber is taken to the _____.

DOWN:
1) The _____ of the religion of the Parsis was Zoroaster.
3) The rest of the food is _____ among those at the priest's house.
7) The New Year is also known as No Ruz or _____.
8) Khordad Sal is the one of the most _____ days of the Parsis calendar.
10) Seven articles of new _____ are to be worn on this day.
11) All the food is _____ by the priest.
13) Khordad Sal is a _____ celebration for the Parsis.
14) The Zoroastrians were driven from _____ by Muslim Arabs.
16) The celebration of Zoroaster's birth takes _____ on Khordad Sal.

ANSWER KEY

MAIN IDEA vs. SUPPORTING DETAILS

1) S
2) M
3) S
4) M

UNDERSTANDING WHAT YOU READ

1) The Zoroastrians were originally from Persia, which is now known as Iran.
2) The most anticipated day of the Parsis calendar is Khordad Sal, which is also known as Havzoru and No Ruz. It is also the day of the celebration of the birth of Zoroaster.
3) The feast for Khordad Sal is prepared in the house of the village priest.
4) The women bring a list of those in their household over the age of nine so the priest will say a prayer for each of these people.

REMEMBERING DETAILS

1) F   The Zoroastrians were driven from Persia by Muslim Arabs.
2) F   Honor is paid to Khordad in the hope that he will bring happiness in the coming year.
3) F   Each women brings a small copper bowl with a melon, a cucumber and an egg inside, as well as a selection of other fruits and vegetable.
4) T

INFERENCES

1) c
2) d

WORD POWER

1) b
2) a
3) b
4) c
5) a
6) b

CROSSWORD PUZZLE

ACROSS: 2) copper 4) melon 5) origins 7) Frawardin 9) respect 12) household 15) temple

DOWN: 1) founder 3) divided 6) Havzoru 8) anticipated 10) clothing 11) blessed 13) special 14) Persia 16) place

Chinese New Year

1 Over one billion people of Chinese descent are spread out in countries around the world. As a result, Chinese New Year is one of the world's most widely and joyously celebrated holidays. It is a holiday with a history that dates back thousands of years, and today much of the celebration is based on ancient customs and traditions.

2 In Western countries, New Year's Eve is most commonly celebrated on December 31st, the last day of the year on the Gregorian calendar. Chinese New Year, however, is celebrated according to the ancient Lunar calendar, which measured time according to the position of the full moon, the sun and the earth. On the Lunar calendar, Chinese New Year arrives at the time of the second new moon following the winter solstice. This is usually between January 20th and February 19th each year.

3 Many of the holiday traditions surrounding Chinese New Year are based on the ancient Chinese legend of Nien (or Nihn). Nien was a mythical monster that came out of its den to hunt and eat at the end of each year. According to legend, Nien was afraid of the color red, fire and loud noises. To protect themselves, it was customary for the Chinese to paint objects bright red, to shine bright lights and candles and to make noise with drums, gongs and exploding bamboo "crackers."

4 Today firecrackers remain a huge part of Chinese New Year celebrations.

On the eve of the New Year, huge fireworks displays are set off in a symbolic attempt to frighten away devils and evil spirits. These explosions usually end the following morning, but fireworks can be seen throughout the entire two weeks of the Chinese New Year celebrations.

5   In keeping with ancient customs, festivities begin at least twenty-four hours before New Year's Eve. People begin preparing for visitors by sweeping, cleaning and washing their homes. According to tradition, they must not be swept again until the New Year to avoid sweeping away good luck. New Year's Day is a time to play host to family and friends, or to travel to the temples with offerings to the Gods.

6   In Chinatown districts in the world's largest cities, New Year's Day is celebrated in an elaborate fashion. In these cities the local Chinese community plays host to colorful lion and dragon dances in the streets of Chinatown. Paper dragon costumes as long as a full city block are carried along the parade route, followed by paper replicas of fish and birds.

7   Another important aspect of the celebration is food. Guests are invited to dine on vegetarian dishes like lohan chai, or yu sang, which is a mixture of raw fish, vegetables, noodles and seasoning. Tang kwa, or sweet dumplings, are also eaten as an offering to the Jade Emperor who protects families from his home in the spirit world.

8   Many Asian countries celebrate the New Year under a different name. In Taiwan, for example, it is known as Sang-Sin, in Vietnam it is called Tet, and in Korea New Year's Eve becomes Je-Sok. No matter what the name, Chinese New Year is still one of the world's best-known Chinese festivals.

MAIN IDEAS vs. SUPPORTING DETAILS

The following sentences are either Main Ideas or Supporting Details. Put an "M" beside those that are Main Ideas, and an "S" beside those that are Supporting Details.

1) _____ Over one billion people of Chinese descent are spread out in countries around the world.
2) _____ Chinese New Year is a celebration based on ancient customs and traditions.
3) _____ Nien was a mythical monster that came out of its den at the end of each year.
4) _____ Food is an important part of the festivities for Chinese New Year.

UNDERSTANDING WHAT YOU READ

If you can, answer these questions from memory. If you cannot, look back at the article.

1) When is Chinese New Year?

_____

2) How do people prepare for New Year's Eve in China?

_____

3) How is New Year's Day celebrated in the Chinatown districts in some of the world's largest cities?

_____

4) What types of dishes are served for Chinese New Year?

_____

REMEMBERING DETAILS

Write TRUE or FALSE under each statement. If the statement is false, write the statement correctly.

1) In Western countries, New Year's Eve is most commonly celebrated on the last day of the Lunar calendar.

_____

2) Nien was scared of the color yellow, lights and strange noises.

_____

3) Fireworks are used symbolically to chase away evil spirits.

_____

4) Yu sang is eaten as an offering to the Jade Emperor.

_____

INFERENCES

Based on the article, circle the letter of the best sentence completion.

1) Chinese New Year is celebrated between January 20th and February 19th because...

a) the Chinese do not follow the Gregorian calendar.
b) that is when Nien emerges from his den.
c) that is the time of the second new moon following the winter solstice, as measured by the Lunar calendar.
d) that is when it is traditionally celebrated.

2) The Jade Emperor is given an offering of food because...

a) he enjoys tang kwa.
b) he protects families from his home in the spirit world.
c) he is one of the gods honored during Chinese New Year.
d) dining on vegetarian dishes is customary during Chinese New Year.

INTERPRETATION

1) Is it possible for one country's customs and traditions to survive totally unchanged for thousands of years? Discuss with a partner whether this is possible.

2) Write a short composition comparing the traditions of New Year's Eve in Western and Asian countries.

3) Based on the story, write a description of a Chinese New Year parade and then compare your description to that of your classmates. Try to use as many adjectives and adverbs as possible.

WORD POWER

Circle the letter of the word that means the same as the word on the left.

1) descent	a) journey	b) slope	c) ancestry
2) measured	a) limited	b) estimated	c) adjusted
3) customary	a) usual	b) unusual	c) frequent
4) throughout	a) initially	b) occasionally	c) everywhere
5) elaborate	a) improved	b) detailed	c) developed
6) aspect	a) appearance	b) part	c) expression

CROSSWORD PUZZLE

ACROSS:
2) Chinese New Year is celebrated according to the ancient _____ calendar.
6) Chinese New Year is one of the most _____ celebrated holidays in the world.
8) Cities play _____ to colorful lion and dragon dances in the streets of Chinatown.
10) _____ to tradition, their homes must not be swept again until the New Year.
12) There are many _____ traditions surrounding Chinese New Year.
13) On the _____ of Chinese New Year there are huge fireworks displays.
14) The paper dragons are followed by paper _____ of fish and birds.
16) Paper dragons have _____ as long as a full city block.

DOWN:
1) December 31st is the last day of the year on the _____ calendar.
3) On Chinese New Year guests are invited to dine on _____ dishes.
4) New Year's Eve is most _____ celebrated on December 31st in Western countries.
5) Nien was a _____ monster that came out of its den at the end of each year.
7) New Year's arrives at the time of the second new moon following the winter _____.
9) The Chinese used to do things to _____ themselves from Nien.
11) On New Year's Day people make _____ to the Gods at temples.
15) The Jade Emperor protects families from his home in the _____ world.

ANSWER KEY

MAIN IDEA vs. SUPPORTING DETAILS

1) S
2) M
3) S
4 M

UNDERSTANDING WHAT YOU READ

1) Chinese New Year is celebrated according to the Lunar calendar. On the Lunar calendar, Chinese New Year arrives at the time of the second new moon following the winter solstice--usually between January 20th and February 19th each year.
2) People in China begin preparing a day in advance for New Year's Eve by sweeping, cleaning and washing their homes.
3) In Chinatown districts in some of the world's largest cities, New Year's Day is celebrated in an elaborate fashion. In these cities the local Chinese community plays host to colorful lion and dragon dances in the streets of Chinatown. Paper dragon costumes as long as a full city block are carried along the parade route, followed by paper replicas of fish and birds.
4) At New Year's people eat vegetarian dishes, such as lohan chai or yu sang and tang kwa.

REMEMBERING DETAILS

1) F   In Western countries, New Year's Eve is most commonly celebrated on the last day of the Gregorian calendar.
2) F   Nien was scared of the color red, fire and loud noises.
3) T
4) F   Tang kwa is eaten as an offering to the Jade Emperor.

INFERENCES

1) c
2) b

WORD POWER

1) c
2) b
3) a
4) c
5) b
6) b

CROSSWORD PUZZLE

ACROSS: 2) Lunar 6) joyously 8) host 10) according 12) holiday 13) eve 14) replicas 16) costumes

DOWN: 1) Gregorian 3) vegetarian 4) commonly 5) mythical 7) solstice 9) protect 11) offerings 15) spirit